FDR´S FIR

FDR's First Fireside Chat

Public Confidence and the Banking Crisis

AMOS KIEWE

Texas A&M University Press : College Station

The paper used in this book meets the minimum requirements
of the American National Standard for Permanence
of Paper for Printed Library Materials, Z39.48-1984.
Binding materials have been chosen for durability.

Library of Congress Cataloging-in-Publication Data

Kiewe, Amos.
    FDR's first fireside chat : public confidence and the banking crisis /
Amos Kiewe.— 1st ed.
        p. cm. —(Library of presidential rhetoric)
    Includes bibliographical references and index.
    ISBN-13: 978-1-58544-597-4 (cloth : alk. paper)
    ISBN-10: 1-58544-597-5 (cloth : alk. paper)
    ISBN-13: 978-1-58544-607-0 (pbk. : alk. paper)
    ISBN-10: 1-58544-607-6 (pbk. : alk. paper)
        1. Banks and banking—United States—History.   2. Roosevelt,
Franklin D. (Franklin Delano), 1882–1945—Oratory.   3. Finance—
United States.   4. United States—Politics and government—
1933–1945.   I. Title.
HG2461.K54   2007
332.10973'09043—dc22   2006100559

Frontispiece: Franklin D. Roosevelt, delivering the
First Fireside Chat. Courtesy Franklin Delano
Roosevelt Presidential Library

To my son Adam,
who will grow to appreciate
the contents of the books
he proudly displays to his friends

*"Mr. Hoover said that if Roosevelt is elected
grass will grow on streets, and Mr. Roosevelt said that
if Hoover is elected there won't be streets."*
From Kitty Foyle, RKO, 1940

*"Our President took such a dry subject as banking
and made everyone understand it, even the bankers."*
Will Rogers, 1933

*"You don't have a fireside? How, then,
do you listen
to the President's speeches?"*
Groucho Marx, in *A Day at the Races,* 1937

Contents

Preface

The research into Franklin D. Roosevelt's First Fireside Chat was among the most interesting projects I have undertaken. After reading of his first radio address, I realized the particular challenge of writing about a very straightforward and simple speech. As a rhetorical critic specializing in presidential rhetoric, I scratched my head for an analytical perspective. I resolved this challenge once the primary sources revealed that the First Fireside Chat was part of a larger dramatic context—the difficult winter of 1932–33 and the long interregnum period between Roosevelt's successful presidential election in November 8, 1932, and his inauguration on March 4, 1933.

The tension and even animosity between President Herbert Hoover and President-elect Franklin D. Roosevelt made the context of the First Fireside Chat all the more intriguing. Documents in both the Hoover and Roosevelt presidential libraries reveal a unique collaboration between the Treasury officials of the outgoing and incoming administrations. This collaboration and the active role holdovers from the Hoover administration undertook impacted most activities of Roosevelt's first week in office, including closing the banks, instigating the Emergency Banking Act, and drafting the First Fireside Chat. What Hoover had not been able to produce was the necessary rhetorical plan essential for restoring the people's confidence in the banking system and in government. This book tells the story of the First Fireside Chat, the context in which it was constructed, the events leading to the radio address, and the effects it had on the American people and the nation's economy.

In telling this story I was aided by several able individuals whom I wish to thank here: Davis W. Houck, my colleague for many years, whose reading of my writing is always insightful and helpful; Craig

Wright of the Herbert Hoover Presidential Library in West Branch, Iowa, whose searches and advice were critical to finding wonderful primary sources; the staff at the Franklin D. Roosevelt Presidential Library in Hyde Park, New York, and especially Alycia Vivona, for finding important documents necessary for this research; Martin J. Medhurst, for thinking of me when seeking to complete the series on presidential rhetoric; and Mary Lenn Dixon, the editor-in-chief at Texas A&M Press, for her continued support, advice, and encouragement.

Address of President Roosevelt by Radio, Delivered from the White House at 10 P.M., March 12, 1933

My friends:

I want to talk for a few minutes with the people of the United States about banking—to talk with the comparatively few who understand the mechanics of banking, but more particularly with the overwhelming majority of you who use banks for the making of deposits and the drawing of checks. I want to tell you what has been done in the last few days, and why it was done, and what the next steps are going to be. I recognize that the many proclamations from State capitols and from Washington, the legislation, the Treasury regulations, and so forth, couched for the most part in banking and legal terms, ought to be explained for the benefit of the average citizen. I owe this, in particular, because of the fortitude and the good temper with which everybody has accepted the inconvenience and hardships of the banking holiday. And I know that when you understand what we in Washington have been about, I shall continue to have your cooperation as fully as I have had your sympathy and your help during the past week.

First of all, let me state the simple fact that when you deposit money in a bank, the bank does not put the money into a safe deposit vault. It invests your money in many different forms of credit—in bonds, in commercial paper, in mortgages and in many other kinds of loans. In other words, the bank puts your money to work to keep the wheels of industry and of agriculture turning around. A comparatively small part of the money that you put into the bank is kept in currency—an amount which in normal times is wholly sufficient to cover the cash needs of the average citizen. In other words, the total amount of all the currency in the country is only a comparatively small proportion of the total deposits in all the banks of the country.

What, then, happened during the last few days of February and the first few days of March? Because of undermined confidence on the part of the public, there was a general rush by a large portion of our population to turn bank deposits into currency or gold—a rush so great that the soundest banks couldn't get enough currency to meet the demand. The reason for this was that on the spur of the moment it was, of course, impossible to sell perfectly sound assets of a bank and convert them into cash, except at panic prices far below their real value. By the afternoon of March third, a week ago last Friday, scarcely a bank in the country was open to do business. Proclamations closing them, in whole or in part, had been issued by the Governors in almost all the states. It was then that I issued the proclamation providing for the national bank holiday, and this was the first step in the Government's reconstruction of our financial and economic fabric.

The second step, last Thursday, was the legislation promptly and patriotically passed by the Congress confirming my proclamation and broadening my powers so that it became possible in view of the requirement of time to extend the holiday and lift the ban of that holiday gradually in the days to come. This law also gave authority to develop a program of rehabilitation of our banking facilities. And I want to tell our citizens in every part of the Nation that the national Congress—Republicans and Democrats alike—showed by this action a devotion to public welfare and a realization of the emergency and the necessity for speed that it is difficult to match in all our history.

The third stage has been the series of regulations permitting the banks to continue their functions to take care of the distribution of food and household necessities and the payment of payrolls.

This bank holiday, while resulting in many cases in great inconvenience, is affording us the opportunity to supply the currency necessary to meet the situation. Remember that no sound bank is a dollar worse off than it was when it closed its doors last week. Neither is any bank which may turn out not to be in a position for immediate opening. The new law allows the twelve Federal Reserve Banks to issue additional currency on good assets and thus the banks that reopen will be able to meet every legitimate call. The new currency is being sent out by the Bureau of Engraving and Printing in large volume to every part of the country. It is sound currency because it is backed by actual, good assets.

Another question you will ask is this: Why are all the banks not to be reopened at the same time? The answer is simple and I know you will understand it: Your Government does not intend that the history of the past few years shall be repeated. We do not want and will not have another epidemic of bank failures.

As a result, we start tomorrow, Monday, with the opening of banks in the twelve Federal Reserve Bank cities—those banks, which on first examination by the Treasury, have already been found to be all right. That will be followed on Tuesday by the resumption of all other functions by banks already found to be sound in cities where there are recognized clearing houses. That means about two hundred and fifty cities of the United States. In other words, we are moving as fast as the mechanics of the situation will allow us.

On Wednesday and succeeding days, banks in smaller places all through the country will resume business, subject, of course, to the Government's physical ability to complete its survey. It is necessary that the reopening of banks be extended over a period in order to permit the banks to make applications for the necessary loans, to obtain currency needed to meet their requirements, and to enable the Government to make common sense checkups.

Please let me make it clear to you that if your bank does not open the first day you are by no means justified in believing that it will not open. A bank that opens on one of the subsequent days is in exactly the same status as the bank that opens tomorrow.

I know that many people are worrying about State banks that are not members of the Federal Reserve System. There is no occasion for that worry. These banks can and will receive assistance from member banks and from the Reconstruction Finance Corporation. And, of course, they are under the immediate control of the State banking authorities. These State banks are following the same course as the National banks except that they get their licenses to resume business from the State authorities, and these authorities have been asked by the Secretary of the Treasury to permit their good banks to open up on the same schedule as the national banks. And so I am confident that the State Banking Departments will be as careful as the national Government in the policy relating to the opening of banks and will follow the same broad theory.

It is possible that when the banks resume a very few people who have not recovered from their fear may again begin withdrawals. Let me make it clear to you that the banks will take care of all needs, except, of course, the hysterical demands of hoarders, and it is my belief that hoarding during the past week has become an exceedingly unfashionable pastime in every part of our nation. It needs no prophet to tell you that when the people find that they can get their money—that they can get it when they want it for all legitimate purposes—the phantom of fear will soon be laid. People will again be glad to have their money where it will be safely taken care of and where they can use it conveniently at any time. I can assure you, my friends, that it is safer to keep your money in a reopened bank than it is to keep it under the mattress.

The success of our whole national program depends, of course, on the cooperation of the public—on its intelligent support and its use of a reliable system.

Remember that the essential accomplishment of the new legislation is that it makes it possible for banks more readily to convert their assets into cash than was the case before. More liberal provision has been made for banks to borrow on these assets at the Reserve Banks and more liberal provision has also been made for issuing currency on the security of these good assets. This currency is not fiat currency. It is issued only on adequate security, and every good bank has an abundance of such security.

One more point before I close. There will be, of course, some banks unable to reopen without being reorganized. The new law allows the Government to assist in making these reorganizations quickly and effectively and even allows the Government to subscribe to at least a part of any new capital that may be required.

I hope you can see, my friends, from this essential recital of what your Government is doing that there is nothing complex, nothing radical in the process.

We have had a bad banking situation. Some of our bankers had shown themselves either incompetent or dishonest in their handling of the people's funds. They had used the money entrusted to them in speculations and unwise loans. This was, of course, not true in the vast majority of our banks, but it was true in enough of them to shock the people of the United States, for a time, into a sense of insecurity and to put them into a frame of mind where they did not differentiate, but seemed to assume that the acts of a comparative few had tainted them all. And so it became the Government's job to straighten out this situation and do it as quickly as possible. And that job is being performed.

I do not promise you that every bank will be reopened or that individual losses will not be suffered, but there will be no losses that possibly could be avoided; and there would have been more and greater losses had we continued to drift. I can even promise you salvation for some, at least, of the sorely pressed banks. We shall be engaged not merely in reopening sound banks but in the creation of more sound banks through reorganization.

It has been wonderful to me to catch the note of confidence from all over the country. I can never be sufficiently grateful to the people for the loyal support that they have given me in their acceptance of the judgment that has dictated our course, even though all our processes may not have seemed clear to them.

After all, there is an element in the readjustment of our financial system more important than currency, more important than gold, and that is the confidence of the people themselves. Confidence and courage are the essentials of success in carrying out our plan. You people must have faith; you must not be stampeded by rumors or guesses. Let us unite in banishing fear. We have provided the machinery to restore our financial system, and it is up to you to support and make it work.

It is your problem, my friends, your problem no less than it is mine.

Together we cannot fail.[1]

Introduction

At 9 A.M. on March 13, 1933, many banks were opened for the first time since President Franklin D. Roosevelt had declared a bank holiday on March 6. With many appearing at banks' doorsteps ready to deposit cash and gold, it was clear that the banking crisis was over. Given their normal closure during the weekend, banks were not open for eight days, causing much hardship and bringing many to fear for their hard-earned money deposited in banks. But on that crucial morning it was obvious that the banking crisis of the past few months had ended. The signs were unmistakable: The dollar bounced back "spectacularly in relation to other currencies." The stock market opened with trading volumes at a record high. Treasury certificates valued at $800 million, which bankers only days earlier feared would not sell, sold at the highest interest rates since World War I. Some 70 percent of banks reopened immediately, and about three thousand banks opened later. Only about two thousand banks with serious liquidity problems required reorganization, and some never reopened.[1]

The banking crisis could have ended differently, and disastrously, had Roosevelt not closed the banks a week earlier. Concern over individuals' banking accounts brought many to withdraw their money for fear that there would be nothing left in the banks to withdraw. The run on the banks brought panic and the hoarding of money and gold as fear pervaded more rational behavior. The nation's banking system edged dangerously close to a complete collapse of its financial institutions. Closing the banks was necessary to stop the hoarding and allow for an interval during which the government could intervene and seek to solve the crisis. Much was at stake as Roosevelt entered the White House, and much was accomplished in his first week in office. Roosevelt succeeded in replacing fear with confidence by resorting to various measures, but none was more crucial than his address to the nation on the banking crisis.

All told, despite the hardship many suffered, more money was deposited than withdrawn during the first few days of the banks' reopening. The people clearly heeded the president's call for confidence. They listened attentively to his radio address on the banking crisis the night before and acted as he recommended. Many wrote Roosevelt about their reaction to the speech, praising his simple and direct talk, complimenting him on his unique approach to relating to the American people, thanking him for visiting them in their homes, and crediting him for giving them an honest account of the situation.

And much confidence was needed, given the gravity of the situation. The potential for economic disaster was so great that officials from both the Hoover and Roosevelt administrations joined efforts to solve the crisis. Several of Hoover's Treasury officials stayed on and helped Roosevelt put the banking system back on solid footing. Such was the cooperation between the incoming and outgoing administrations. Tensions between Hoover and Roosevelt, which had intensified the banking crisis significantly during the winter of 1932–33, were constructively smoothed by Treasury officials from both administrations for the greater benefit of the nation. Several of Hoover's Treasury officials gave substantial help that reached all aspects of the crisis, including the drafting of the First Fireside Chat.

In that radio address, Roosevelt asked the nation to have confidence in the banks, assuring them that when the banks reopened their deposits would be safe. The objective of the speech was to assure that hoarding of currency and gold would not resume and to restore confidence in the banking system. The speech, only later dubbed a "fireside chat," called for immediate results. It was a crucial speech with the most pressing objectives, and it yielded the results sought. The First Fireside Chat would enter the annals of great speeches. History would treat the speech favorably, despite its lack of eloquence. The speech is not adorned with flourish, does not incorporate impressive metaphors, and does not carry memorable lines. It is rather simple, quite straightforward, and almost technical. Unlike so many presidential speeches, this one actually had to do something "right now." It was a most instrumental address—and it succeeded very materially. Perhaps this is one reason it makes the "greatest" lists, in addition to the fact that it was "first" in the genre of firesides. It is one of the most important speeches in U.S. history, and this is its story.

Franklin D. Roosevelt delivered his First Fireside Chat on Sunday, March 12, 1933, at the end of one of the most volatile weeks in U.S. history. A week earlier, on March 4, he had been inaugurated the thirty-second president of the United States. Throughout the first week in office, Roosevelt faced one of the most ominous financial crises the nation had ever experienced, threatening to topple the U.S. economy and bring the country to a complete collapse. Few presidents faced such a precarious first week; perhaps only Lincoln's was more daunting. Deteriorating economic developments in Europe and their political consequences in Hitler's Germany and Mussolini's Italy would usher in a most dangerous course of events.

After the First Fireside Chat, confidence in the banks' solvency quickly spread around the nation, as demonstrated by the amount of money, gold bullion, and gold certificates redeposited in them. The many letters private citizens sent Roosevelt also illustrate how well the nation received his radio address. Alvin C. Zurcher of Chillicothe, Ohio, wrote for many by covering much ground in his short letter to the president. He congratulated Roosevelt on his "inspiring address over the radio" and suggested that "such an arrangement would be tremendously helpful not only to the President but to the nation. It will enable you to bring your leadership and helpful personality direct to the citizen in his own living room where you may chat confidentially with him for

10 or 15 minutes. Having secured the confidence and following of the people with your brave leadership, you now have a golden opportunity to retain it and even to foster it to greater proportions."[2] Mr. Zurcher touched on the critical issue of confidence, Roosevelt's leadership skills, the intimate nature of radio broadcasting, and the quality of the speech. Notwithstanding the naïveté of assuming the confidentiality of a radio talk, his letter illustrates the novelty of Roosevelt's rhetorical skills and the radio medium as a perfect vehicle for his presidency.

The challenges Roosevelt faced in confronting the banking crisis are part of a larger context of economic turmoil that began some four years earlier when the stock market crashed. Yet even in 1929 the crisis was not as severe as in the winter of 1932–33. Throughout the interim period between November 8, 1932, when Roosevelt was elected president, and his assumption of office some four months later, the United States experienced a worsening financial situation, which reached a critical point by February 1933, when domestic and foreign interests began to withdraw money and gold in large amounts from U.S. banks, literally depleting the nation of its capital reserves and causing massive bank failures.

Roosevelt's first radio address would be given at the conclusion of a week replete with rhetorical maneuvering, especially his pivotal inaugural address.[3] In addition, Roosevelt closed all banks by declaring a bank holiday on March 6, managed to meet gathering state governors, held a press conference, issued public statements, got an emergency banking bill passed by Congress in one day, extended the bank holiday, and, finally, delivered the radio address. All these political acts also carried a rhetorical function—ensuring the American people that their new president was acting fast to solve the banking crisis, and that when the banks reopened the hoarding would stop and banks would resume solvency and normal operations. The radio address explicitly asked people to stop hoarding money and gold and even return those funds already withdrawn. And indeed, not only did people stop hording money and gold, they brought back their money and gold bullion, reversing a dangerous course and saving capitalism.

That the First Fireside Chat was successful is an easy conclusion. But how did Roosevelt do that? How was he able to persuade people to reverse course? How could he do this in such a short time? What was in the "chat" that brought people to stop fearing? How did he manage to do this in the context of high anxiety and fear? And to what degree were Hoover's failures Roosevelt's successes?

In this book I seek to answer these questions by telling the story of the First Fireside Chat, including the events that led to the financial crisis, the pressure put on Roosevelt by Herbert Hoover during the interregnum period, the banking crisis, the Treasury's plan to avert the crisis, and Roosevelt's rhetorical plan culminating in the radio address that saved the nation from financial collapse.

The story of the First Fireside Chat has a beginning, but like all beginnings some arbitrary date is necessary in order to make sense of the progression of events. This story begins on November 10, 1932, when Great Britain asked the United States to defer its World War I debt payment due November 15. It also requested that the entire debt issue be "reviewed," a diplomatic euphemism for considering debt forgiveness.[4] This request was alarming enough that President Hoover cut short his California vacation and headed back to the nation's capital. On his way back east, Hoover sent president-elect Franklin D. Roosevelt a message describing the recent development and suggested that the two confer in Washington D.C. Hoover thought that he needed the president-elect's help, given his own limitation as a lame duck president, a lame duck Congress, and the prospects that such negotiations with debtor nations would be extended into the next administration.

Roosevelt, who had won the presidential election only days earlier, initially agreed to meet with Hoover. Perhaps naïve about the president's request, Roosevelt was quickly cautioned by some of his close advisers not to commit too early, especially since the elections would increase the number of Democrats in the next Congress. Roosevelt, then, would have to find a way to distance himself from Hoover yet appear cooperative. To manage the delicate negotiation with Hoover, Roosevelt would cite lack of constitutional authority to do anything until his inauguration on March 4, 1933. Thus began a difficult and quite strange interregnum dance that lasted four months, during which the economic situation worsened and Hoover became increasingly frustrated and even desperate with Roosevelt's reluctance to do what he requested. Despite several meetings between the two, Roosevelt consistently refused to commit himself. He could not accede to Hoover's requests, at least not to the degree that Hoover wished.

It would be shortsighted, though, to fault Roosevelt. After all, Hoover expected too much, to say the least. He did not just ask the president-elect to meet and exchange ideas, he actually asked him to commit to Republican policies and Republican principles.[5] Historian David M. Kennedy considers Hoover's request for Roosevelt's help to "contain sinister political implications."[6] Roosevelt clearly could not have accepted a Republican dictate, regardless of the severity of the financial crisis. There is also some credence to the suspicion that Hoover was not thinking economically but politically. Indeed, Hoover's secretary of state (and Roosevelt's colleague from the Wilson administration), Henry Stimson, opined that Hoover was seeking to vindicate his presidency and policies by "recruiting" Roosevelt.[7] Such was the state of affairs between the president and the president-elect.

The larger context for the growing financial crisis was sown several years earlier, both domestically and internationally. As early as 1926, Roosevelt was warning of growing economic difficulties resulting primarily from the disparities between urban and rural economies, the foreclosure of many family farms, and the decline in farm prices.[8] Another variable in the growing domestic problem was the rise of small, local, and poorly regulated banks that forwarded many farm loans. Many of these "mom and pop" banks lacked the securities and collateral necessary for sound banking.[9]

With a lack of proper supervision, bankers, both small and large, were prone to unsound and less than ethical practices. Scandals began to surface, and disclosure before various congressional committees revealed the extent of the corruption: a Wall Street bank that loaned money at no interest to its own officers to protect them against a stock market crash; a banker who sold stocks to his depositors without revealing to them that he also charged their account against the stock sale.[10] Such incidents brought suspicion and distrust that furthered the perception that depositors' money was unsafe in the banks.

Bank foreclosures grew alarming. In 1931, 2,290 banks closed doors, 1,772 of them not members of the Federal Reserve System.[11] Testifying before the Committee on Ways and Means of the House of Representatives on April 28 and 29, 1932, Eugene Meyer, governor of the Federal Reserve Board, stated the following: "Personally I feel, as I stated to a subcommittee of the Banking and Currency Committee the other day, that we will never have a satisfactory banking system in the United States until banks of deposit, commercial banks, can be gathered under one charting, supervising and regulatory power. The constant competition between State and national banking systems has resulted in a weakening of the laws and the safeguards of both systems."[12]

The international scene was pivotal in the ensuing crisis. Financial breakdown of the Credit Anstalt in Vienna in 1931 and England's decision to abandon the gold standard on September 21, 1931, were ominous signs.[13] One of the key differences between the president and the president-elect was Hoover's international focus. Confidence in the economic market, Hoover thought, could be restored by attending to Europe's debt reparations, maintaining the gold standard, and balancing the national budget. Thus, he sought cooperation with European allies, though with limited comprehension of larger concerns such as growing nationalism in Europe and the disruption of the economies of several European countries. And as world markets began to collapse, Hoover failed to focus on the political reasons for the economic downturn as well as specific economic issues such as high U.S. tariffs. Instead, "the Hoover-Mills policies stressed . . . a purely financial approach on the assumption that confidence would then be restored elsewhere." Hoover's rude awakening occurred in the summer of 1931 when central banks in Europe, especially in Germany, were on the verge of collapse.[14] In his State of the Union address on December 8, 1931, Hoover announced that "the chief influence affecting the state of the Union during the past year has been the continued worldwide economic disturbance."[15] Roosevelt would subscribe to a different perspective altogether, pointing to the "collapse of agriculture income and purchasing power" as the root cause of the depression.[16]

These disparate perspectives would figure prominently later as two influential groups of advisers sought to sway Roosevelt to adopt either an international perspective or a domestic perspective on how to solve the Depression and growing financial and banking crisis. That the international perspective was closely allied with the Hoover administration is ironic given that the Hoover Treasury officials who stayed on during the early days of the Roosevelt administration and worked on all the details of the bank holiday, the banking emergency act, and the First Fireside Chat would emphasize domestic solutions.

Banking failure continued into 1932, and in January 1932 alone some 342 banks closed their doors. To head off further banking failure, a new government agency was created, the Reconstruction Finance Corporation (RFC), authorized to loan "adequate securities" to all classes of banks. With the establishment of the RFC, the number of bank failures fell in March to about 46, but in May and June the failures increased again. The RFC loan of some $90 million to the Central Republic National Bank of Chicago, a key bank in Illinois, was taken as a serious development and increased perception of endemic banking problems throughout the nation. To forestall additional banking failures, the Glass-Steagall Act of February 27, 1932, authorized the use of Federal Reserve bank notes as security (in the form of government bonds) to assist weak banks. By July 1932, these measures seem to have quieted the financial markets.[17]

The situation worsened, however, immediately after Roosevelt won the presidential election on November 8, 1932. More banks were forced to close, but this time the culprit may have been political and perceptual. Two particular developments may have caused the fiscal crisis to intensify. One was the insistence by the Speaker of the House and vice president-elect Garner to publish RFC loans in the press. This plan added pressure on banks, both strong and weak, to detail loans taken and justify their need. Such revelations further intensified the perception of unsound banking. The other was talk that the Roosevelt administration might depreciate the dollar.[18] The plan of the incoming Roosevelt administration was for a "sound currency," a euphemism for a cheaper dollar and inflationary forces necessary to increase commodities' prices, increased productivity and resumption of normal employment rates, measures that the incoming administration deemed necessary for the restoration of fiscal and economic stability. Of all of these proposed measures, the one Hoover resented and feared the most was the abandonment of the gold standard.[19]

At the Intersection of Rhetoric and Economics

The banks' failure of 1933 was largely perceptual, promulgated by fear of impending banking collapse and a lack of credible statements that most banks were safe and solvent. The story of the First Fireside Chat, then, is largely a rhetorical one in that words and only words changed human behavior and action. This particular rhetorical story is situated in the larger context of economic behavior where human perceptions are detrimental to economic behavior. This perspective, which espouses a study of economics that is less about numbers and predictions then about the intangibles of fear and confidence, often runs counter to the more prevailing scientific perspective.

Confidence in the economy, as tautological as it may sound, is the key to economic viability. Economic markets function well when people have confidence in the financial market, and such confidence is realized when capital is used to advance economic growth; when both individuals and institutions invest because they believe that the investment will yield the sought returns; when people put their money in the bank, trusting that it will grow and be available when needed; and when banks believe that their loans for entrepreneurial purposes will be returned and the investment prove profitable.

The principal idea of putting money away or giving it to someone else for trust or management is based on faith in those handling the money. Absent such faith, no economic system can maintain its viability and no nation can become successful. Faith and confidence are essential ingredients of any economy. These economic ingredients are, however, not tangible but rhetorical and perceptual in the sense that institutions and markets project credibility essential for successful economic transactions, political leaders engage in persuasive acts in reaching domestic and international audiences about investment opportunities, and financial and banking institutions manage commodity transfer via their long-standing reputations as honest brokers.

In March 1933, in the midst of the financial and economic crisis, an essay in *Harpers Magazine* expressed this very sentiment of economic confidence. In an acute and perceptive way, the essay considered the loss of confidence "a phenomenon of mass psychology." It noted that neither "the loss of confidence nor the restoration of confidence is a subjective process. . . . It is merely an instinctive reaction to external things; specifically, to some compelling economic event, some change or sign of change in economic order."[20]

In his study *Rhetoric as Currency: Hoover, Roosevelt and the Great Depression,* Davis W. Houck observes that "some who claim the mantle of economic experts would have us believe that the economy is a tangible, living entity, a thing that can be accurately described and observed—even predicted." Instead, Houck argues that "'faith' . . . is the master metaphor that accompanies much of the talk about economics." Relying on John Maynard Keynes, Houck emphasizes the "immaterial" and "animal spirits" in economic behavior, where "public opinion, and the alleviation of fear, doubt, and precariousness" are more detrimental to a nation's economy than scientific measurements. The treatises on economic behavior by Keynes, as well John Kenneth Galbraith and Deirdre McCloskey, bring Houck to point to "rhetoric as palpable currency: thought, beliefs, and emotions constitute and create our economic realities; and markets are propped up on the edifice of discourse." Finally, Houck meticulously traces the weight both presidents gave to the intangibles of confidence rhetoric in seeking to bring economic recovery. What is perhaps quite revealing is the degree to which Hoover and Roosevelt both practiced the rhetoric of economics long before it would become an academic pursuit.[21] Perhaps Adam Smith's invisible hand might very well be a rhetorical hand.

Preview

The study of presidential rhetoric calls for a critical view that can shed light on the working of words and their impact on the polity. It requires careful reading of primary and secondary texts, a critical eye, and rhetorical and critical theories that may help explain a rhetorical text, its antecedent events, context, constraints, and results. My reading of Roosevelt's First Fireside Chat is aided by situating the speech in the historical and economic context of the banking crisis, which I develop by close scrutiny of many memoranda, letters, drafts of speeches, memoirs, and diaries deposited in presidential libraries and other archives. To complete this comprehensive study of the First Fireside Chat, I assess the speech against audience reaction and feedback, consulting the many letters written to Roosevelt as well as the assessing press comments on the speech.

In developing the story of the First Fireside Chat, I pay close attention to the progression of events that led to the construction of the radio address of March 12, 1933. In chapter 1, I describe Roosevelt's talent in bringing radio broadcasting to the political arena and focus on one particular radio address, "The Forgotten Man," a speech that both stylistically and substantively does much to foreshadow the First Fireside Chat. Chapter 2 presents the political and economic context for the growing banking crisis, highlighting the developing plan for solving the crisis during the interregnum between the Hoover and Roosevelt administrations. In chapter 3, I examine the crucial final months of the Hoover administration when a run on the banks brought the United States to the verge of financial collapse. This chapter highlights the many early efforts to solve the banking crisis, with key Treasury officials crafting the plan to close the banks and doing so in partial cooperation with the incoming administration, though hampered by a cautious outgoing president. In chapters 4 and 5, I discuss Roosevelt's actions as he assumed office, beginning with the crucial decision to declare a bank holiday and following through the frantic work of key aides and several Hoover Treasury officials who stayed on to finalize the necessary Emergency Banking Act and to help draft the First Fireside

Chat. Chapter 6 begins with the controversy regarding who drafted the First Fireside Chat and moves through a comprehensive analysis of the speech. Chapter 7 documents the reaction to the First Fireside Chat, especially as displayed in the letters private citizens wrote Roosevelt immediately after listening to the radio address. With chapter 8, I bring this book to closure by assessing the First Fireside Chat and its impact on the nation. This chapter includes a postscript describing the departure of the key Hoover officials from the Roosevelt administration once the banking crisis dissipated.

CHAPTER 1

Radio Roosevelt

Franklin D. Roosevelt was an innovator; he liked to experiment, sought new ideas, and was not bound by the tried and true. Above all else, Roosevelt was a progressive thinker. No wonder he adopted radio early on. Roosevelt and radio were perfect for each other. Roosevelt became a prospective president when he was elected New York's governor just as radio was becoming a household feature. Radio sets in the United States increased from some three million in 1924 to thirty million by 1936. Two years later, 91 percent of all urban homes and 70 percent of all rural homes had a radio set. The radio in the 1930s became an important focal point in one's home and "a highly valued and permanent piece of living room furniture, and an integral part of family life."[1]

Roosevelt's physical disability no doubt helped him realize the power of the medium as ideal for an immobile politician, able to reach millions with relative ease. As governor of New York he had used radio broadcasts to reach many—and to do so over the heads of the state legislature when he became annoyed by its rejection of his proposed bills. His first radio address was broadcast in 1929 as a means to battle "a recalcitrant legislature."[2] He opted to "take the issue to the people," and radio was the perfect medium for such a strategy.

The reaction to his first radio address was overwhelming, with a large quantity of mail arriving in Albany decisively supportive of the governor.[3] The opposition would become quite apprehensive of Roosevelt's radio addresses, because the governor excelled in "his persuasive mastery over that intimate medium," and he did so "without editorial comment from an intervening press."[4]

Roosevelt was able to achieve great success with the use of radio as a political tool because he was born with a gifted voice. His mother attributed his good voice to the Delano side. His radio delivery was pleasing, and he enjoyed a highly expressive intonation and inflection that allowed for an effective conversational style.[5] Historian Alonzo Hamby considers Roosevelt to have possessed "perhaps the finest radio voice of an era in which the medium became the vehicle of political mass communication"[6] And though one tends to distinguish voice from character, and indeed Roosevelt had "the best modulated radio voice in public life,"[7] we should not separate his vocal quality from his character. Indeed, "his hearers felt the warmth of regard for all persons expressed through the medium of his voice, but many, without analysis, attributed the warmth to his voice alone, neglecting its more fundamental basis in personality."[8]

Roosevelt would deliver roughly three hundred radio addresses, only some of them considered "fireside chats." He used the radio medium to persuade a majority of the American people to accept his domestic and foreign policy agendas, and to support his personal political ambitions. Roosevelt was quite in awe of the power of radio over people's lives and noted to one radio executive that "nothing since the creation of the newspaper has had so profound an effect on our civilization as radio." Radio in the United States afforded Roosevelt flexibility not realized in Europe, where new dictators such as Hitler turned the medium into a state propaganda machine. Radio in the United States was not much regulated, unlike newspapers in the 1930s, allowing Roosevelt to promote his political aspirations above the more partisan and controlled press.[9]

Roosevelt showed politicians everywhere the effective use of radio, allowing him to become "one of the greatest performers American radio has had. His dramatic range was wide." As many letter writers would state, they were "vastly entertained, comforted, enlightened, roused to partisan glee, or patriotically inspired, depending on the speech they

heard."[10] Roosevelt's First Fireside Chat was perfectly timed, coming
about when radio reached public prominence; it had matured into a
mode of publicness while American political parties had been in decline
since the turn of the century. David M. Ryfe explains that the "mode
of publicness" refers to form and not to content of public interactions,
and that discourse in the context of the radio medium meant the use
of an easygoing, conversational, and friendly style. This preferred style
explains the frequent use of "I," "you," and "we" to develop a special
relationship between the people and their president. More important,
Roosevelt's radio addresses asked the people to develop their identity—albeit in line with Roosevelt's prescriptions. The radio broadcasts
were suggestive, offering a prototype citizenry—patriotic, heroic, brave,
and independent. In this way, Roosevelt was able to reduce complex
issues to the psychological state of individuals.[11]

Roosevelt developed his radio addresses for a vast audience, re-
quiring him to find a language that appealed to many citizens and
avoided alienating anyone. He thus used simple words, choosing from
a limited number of some "1,000 most common words in the English
language."[12]

The context of the banking crisis would be ideal for such an approach, since the solution to the crisis rested completely on public
psychology. Later Roosevelt would turn fireside chats into media events
that monopolized radio time, preempted other broadcasts, and allowed
him unprecedented access and the ability to mobilize the American
people. His radio appeal was based on his ability to employ "the gram-
mar of mass culture in his fireside chats to close the gap between him
and his mass audience," thereby leading the audience to attend primarily
to Roosevelt's performance.[13] In other words, rhetorical performance
stood for leadership and action.

"The Forgotten Man"

One of the most successful speeches Roosevelt gave as governor of New
York was a radio address strategically titled "The Forgotten Man." This
address, a key campaign speech, is important for understanding and

appreciating the First Fireside Chat and Roosevelt's approach to the banking crisis. It was a radio address, and a very successful one. It was the last radio address Roosevelt delivered before assuming the presidency. And it focused on the economic turmoil engulfing the nation and included specific statements about the growing banking crisis.

Less than a year before he became president, Roosevelt touched on the main issues of the growing economic and banking crises, and his prognosis is rather surprising considering his later policies and rhetoric during the first week in the White House. "The Forgotten Man" speech outlined some of the principles Roosevelt would apply to solving the banking crisis, even before the crisis worsened dramatically in a matter of months. It concentrated on the economic crisis and forwarded a simple analysis of the causes of the emergency. This address is significant given Roosevelt's criticism of the Hoover administration and his own solutions to the economic situation once he assumed the presidency.

Roosevelt's theme of the "Forgotten Man" was appealing. His style and tone complemented the appeal to the common citizen, and the extensive use of "I" in the initial paragraphs gave the speech a conversational flavor, transforming the radio address into a chat between a governor and his neighbors. From the very title, Roosevelt sought to side with the many downtrodden who continued to suffer under the Great Depression. The objective of the speech was clearly to distinguish two approaches, two philosophies, and two individuals: Republican and Democrat, the uncaring and the sufferers, Hoover and Roosevelt.

Roosevelt anchored his speech on his experience with World War I, when the entire nation combined forces to engage in a successful war and overcome an emergency. Today, Roosevelt opined, the nation was facing a greater emergency than the one in 1917. Yet, just as Napoleon lost the Battle of Waterloo because he forgot his infantry, "the present Administration in Washington provides a close parallel. It has either forgotten or it does not want to remember the infantry of our economic army." Couched in war metaphors, Roosevelt used vivid military imagery that would serve him later when closing the banks was rationalized as akin to a war emergency. And in this emergency, claimed Roosevelt, the present administration forgot its most valued weapon—the arsenal of people as the most "indispensable units of economic power." Unlike the current administration in Washington, Roosevelt would not forget the common man and neither would he lose faith in the "forgotten man at the bottom of the economic pyramid."[14] In "The Forgotten Man," as in many other speeches, Roosevelt also sought to dispel any notion of being unfit for the highest office because of his physical disability, the result of contracting polio in 1921. The rhetoric of vibrancy and the metaphors of war and battle were purposeful and would serve him well in countering any notion that he was physically limited and unfit for political office.[15]

The unthinking Hoover, argued Roosevelt, turned to the illusions of economic magic in the form of a major infusion of currency into the system. This would not work, Roosevelt suggested. Creating public work projects would help very few and, at best, they could serve as a stopgap. Neither would the public works help where the problems lie—in the farms and farming. The "real economic cure must go to the killing of bacteria in the system rather than to the treatment of external symptoms." Dr. Roosevelt, who would later use public work projects such as the Tennessee Valley Authority, chastised the Hoover administration for proposing the very same thing. Like a good physician, Roosevelt would attack the root causes and not their symptoms. And the root cause in Roosevelt's analysis was farming, on which roughly fifty million people, about half of the population, depended for their livelihoods. The crisis in farming was the result of reduced prices of produce, thus making farming a losing enterprise. The problem was caused by the imbalance of having too many people reside in cities and employed in industrial firms. Their manufactured products could not be sold to farmers who enjoyed no profit and had no purchasing power. Echoing Lincoln's "house divided" speech, Roosevelt stated that "no nation can long continue half bankrupt."[16]

The solution, then, was clear: raise the purchasing power of farmers and ensure that they remain on their farms instead of allowing bank foreclosures. Roosevelt also counted among the forgotten the "local lender," who did not wish to evict the farmer from his land but was forced to do so in order to keep his small bank solvent. "His [Roosevelt's generic farmer] relationship to the great banks of Chicago and New York is pretty remote. The two billion dollar fund which President Hoover and the Congress have put at the disposal of the big banks, the railroads and the corporations of the nation is not for him. His is a relationship to his little local bank or local loan company." As events unfolded during late winter and early spring 1933, it became clear that a significant cause of the banking crisis was the many unregulated small banks. Roosevelt the defender of the forgotten farmer would concentrate some eleven months later on the soundness and liquidity of big banks and close forever some mom-and-pop banks because they were not sound. But in the "Forgotten Man" speech, Roosevelt championed the cause of "the little fellow" and small banks and chastised the interests of the large banks and corporations.[17]

Roosevelt also identified high tariffs as a cause for the Great Depression, suggesting that tariff policy must be based on "economic common sense rather than upon politics—hot air—pull." The Hawley-Smoot Tariff bill, in Roosevelt's opinion, was the culmination of fences built so high that they decreased world trade and in some cases eliminated it altogether. Although factories ran at 80 percent capacity, there were no buyers for the products inside the United States, and to sell goods abroad required foreign buyers to have money for their purchase. But foreign buyers did not have that kind of money; they could purchase items only by reciprocal exchange of goods. However, "this foolish tariff of ours makes that impossible." The solution, Roosevelt advised, was to reconstruct the tariff policy, to restore the farmers' buying power, and to provide relief to small banks. Roosevelt was clearly arguing against Hoover's international perspective, taking on the president by refuting the very stance of the Republican administration.[18]

Roosevelt also attacked Hoover on the human level, stating that he was not convinced that the Hoover administration would show any concern for the "forgotten man," their only concern being for those at "the top of the social and economic structure." The current administration, Roosevelt stated, failed to plan ahead and instead waited until "something has cracked and then at the last moment have sought to prevent total collapse."[19]

Roosevelt's ending is instructive: "It is high time to get back to fundamentals. It is high time to admit with courage that we are in the midst of an emergency at least equal to that of war. Let us mobilize to meet it."[20] Roosevelt developed a thesis that would both help him several months later but also contradict some of his solutions. Many of his arguments were precursors to those used later in his campaign for the presidency. Several arguments here would appear again in his first inaugural address and in the First Fireside Chat. Roosevelt hinted at deflating the currency by getting off the gold standard in order to strengthen the purchasing power of farmers and thus restart the nation's economic engines. But the defender of the small bank would side later with big banks, putting the banking system on a solid footing and preventing future banking crises. The analogy of the economic emergency with war was not merely analogy; both Hoover and Roosevelt were later advised that the 1917 Trading with the Enemy Act could actually be used to close the banks. The war imagery also allowed Roosevelt to "mobilize" and "lead" an army, a popular one for sure. And though a war metaphor seems incongruent with the forgotten man and his many hardships, Roosevelt, the caring leader, used it to persuade many that he was physically able to lead the nation in the context of the growing economic emergency. Finally, this early radio address exhibits straightforward and simple explanations for complex economic issues. The governor of New York was clearly positioning himself for national leadership.

"The Forgotten Man" would be remembered immediately after the broadcast of the First Fireside Chat on March 12, 1933. Many who wrote letters to Roosevelt in reaction to the later speech highlighted "The Forgotten Man" radio address as the speech that for them commenced a special relationship with the president, and they reminded Roosevelt that they *had* been with him since the earlier radio address.

The Winter of Discontent

The interregnum period from Election Day of November 8, 1932, to Inauguration Day on March 4, 1933, brought the three-year old Depression to a precarious and even dangerous level. The U.S. economy faltered badly, nearing collapse as an additional three million people joined the unemployment role from a year earlier.[1] The two protagonists, Herbert Hoover and Franklin D. Roosevelt, would exacerbate the economic crisis. Roosevelt's election to the presidency commenced a rhetorical dance initiated by lame duck Hoover, who sought Roosevelt's help in diffusing the economic crisis while at same time seeking to have the president-elect abandon the very program that propelled him to the presidential election.

The immediate financial crisis was exacerbated only days after Roosevelt won the presidential election. Hoover informed the president-elect that the debt owed to the United States by France and Great Britain "would not be forthcoming," though a month later Britain did pay the United States the $95 million it owed.[2] France, however, defaulted on its payment. Hoover would use the foreign debt as leverage to bring Britain and France back to the gold standard—the real economic culprit in his view. Roosevelt, who was counseled by two different teams of advisers, wavered between the advice of internationalists Norman Davis (Hoover's representative to the Disarmament Conference and previously undersecretary of state under Wilson) and Henry Stimson (Hoover's secretary of state), on one hand, and that of domestic-conscious "Brain Trusters" Raymond Moley and Rexford Tugwell, on the other.[3]

Political affiliation of individuals in both the Hoover and Roosevelt camps portended Roosevelt's first week in office and the First Fireside Chat. Davis was a fiscally conservative Democrat and leaned to the Republican worldview, and Stimson enjoyed easy access to Roosevelt. Both Davis and Stimson pressured Roosevelt to accept Hoover's emphasis on the international component of the fiscal crisis.[4] Moley, the most powerful adviser to Roosevelt during the interregnum period and the early weeks of the his presidency, together with Tugwell, focused on domestic issues and sought to ensure that Roosevelt did not abandon the New Deal. With much diplomatic skill and great tenacity, Moley in particular was able to keep Roosevelt attentive to the domestic agenda.[5] Consequently, Roosevelt refused to commit himself to any of Hoover's requests but kept the appearance of cooperation and conferred with Hoover throughout the winter of 1932–33.

The clear proof that Roosevelt sided with the domestic New Deal agenda came in a statement to a group of progressives: "The only thing for the United States to do as far as Europe was concerned was to withdraw into its shell and sit still until we regain our economic power."[6] Similarly, in his March 4 inaugural address, Roosevelt stated that "our international trade relations, though vastly important, are in point of time and necessity secondary to the establishment of a sound economy."[7]

The disparate views on the nature of the financial crisis at hand conditioned the perspectives taken to solve it. In Moley's view, there were two crises: a debt crisis and a banking crisis. In Hoover's view, the crisis was over foreign debt owed to the United States and thus was international in nature. Davis W. Houck argues that, although the debt crisis was fiscal in orientation, the banking crisis was largely rhetorical, born of fear and spreading quickly, thus necessitating primarily a rhetorical solution in the form of instilling confidence. Indeed, Roosevelt would approach the banking crisis as rhetorical, thus ensuring a successful resolution, while Hoover, caught in the very paradigm he created for understanding the crisis, could not go beyond its technicalities and thus failed to solve it. Hoover invited Roosevelt to a meeting in the White House on November 22, 1932, and informed him that he wished to renegotiate the debt agreement in order to prevent further international economic panic. However, such renegotiation with France and Great Britain would be difficult unless Congress supported Hoover, which seemed unlikely given Congress's decision the previous year not to renegotiate foreign debt. Roosevelt politely declined to help, citing his status as a private citizen with no authority in the matter.[8]

Another meeting called by Hoover took place on January 20, 1933, with Moley and Davis accompanying the president-elect. Hoover again sought Roosevelt's support for his plan to renegotiate the debt issue with Great Britain. Moley claims that he found himself fighting a lone battle for Roosevelt, with no help from Davis or from Roosevelt. Moley wanted to keep the foreign debt and economic issues separate, whereas Hoover, Mills, and Stimson sought to privilege the international dimension of the crisis.[9]

Hoover's concern over the gold standard as the sine qua non of economic recovery both at home and abroad was the very stumbling block the president could not overcome. The administration's concern over maintaining the gold standard was well displayed in the Treasury's activities during the winter of 1932–33. In his January 25, 1933, diary entry, Moley describes an interesting account of William Woodin, soon to be Roosevelt's first secretary of the treasury and a person with good connections to the Republican Party who went snooping around at the Hoover Treasury. At the Treasury, Woodin learned that George Harrison, governor of the Federal Reserve Bank in New York, was planning to go to Great Britain "to sound them out and to bring back reports of the state of mind over there."[10] Presumably, Governor Harrison wanted a firsthand account of Britain's readiness to resume the gold standard. However, Eugene Meyer, chairman of the Federal Reserve Board, refused to allow Harrison to travel. Chairman Meyer, according to Moley's papers, "has never gone all the way with the Hoover crowd."[11]

Moley's account of the unusual way Woodin learned of this development is most intriguing. Woodin "was putting on his rubbers when he overheard Harrison talking to someone else about it. Harrison was much abashed when he saw Woodin there; but there was nothing for him to do but tell him the whole story." "There is little doubt," Moley writes in his diary, "that the desire of Harrison to go [to England] is connected in some way with the game that is being played in this debt situation." Woodin also confided that he learned from Harrison that Senator Carter Glass was hesitant to accept Roosevelt's proposal that he take the Treasury position because he wanted Roosevelt to state clearly his opposition to inflationary measures.[12] What is important in these accounts is the degree to which the Hoover administration focused on the gold standard as essential to economic recovery and sound banking, and the fear that Roosevelt would devalue the dollar and abandon the gold standard altogether in order to allow inflationary measures that in turn would increase prices and restart economic engines.[13]

Roosevelt, however, would not rule out an inflationary move and told Moley to "make it perfectly clear that so far as subordinates go . . . we are not going to throw ideas out of the window simply because they are labeled inflationary."[14] Roosevelt's vague statements on inflationary measures were correctly interpreted as the planned abandonment of the gold standard. The winter of 1933 was spent largely fighting over the gold standard, with Hoover continuously seeking to move Roosevelt away from such a plan.

Viewing the crisis from the limited perspective of the international scene caused Hoover to ignore other causes. Specifically, Hoover considered the debt owed to the United States by Great Britain, France, and Italy after World War I as the core of the problem and the need to return to the gold standard as the necessary vehicle for stopping the economic downturn and restoring stability. For Britain to return to the gold standard it would first have to pay its debts.[15] Roosevelt's hints throughout 1932 that he would take the United States off the gold standard complicated this issue for Hoover, who argued that for this very reason international markets began to act nervously and commenced the withdrawal of gold from the United States.

From Hoover's perspective, given his lame duck constraints and a narrow margin of Democrats in the House, his requests for Roosevelt's intervention made sense, but only up to a point. Hoover knew that he could not pass the necessary legislation with Democrats in the majority in Congress. Indeed, his proposals for a budget cut of $544 million and a 2.25 percent tax on manufactured products were rejected.[16] Waiting patiently and working behind the scenes, Roosevelt ingratiated himself with Congress in order to build the momentum for his New Deal legislation.[17] Hoover, however, wanted Roosevelt to do much more than just help the situation. He wanted Roosevelt to commit to Republican policies, and that the president-elect could not do.

Though Hoover sought Roosevelt's help on several occasions during the interregnum, the call for such intervention increased from February until Inauguration Day. Hoover's principal objective was to have Roosevelt issue statements throughout the winter of 1932–33 that would "quiet the panic."[18] A strange and revealing consistency operated in Hoover, who by June 1932, before the Democratic convention, was arguing that electing Roosevelt would bring panic to economic markets.[19] Was Hoover trapped in his own paradigm, or did he dislike Roosevelt so much that he could not see beyond the personal animosity? This animosity would prove detrimental to Hoover through the final hours of his presidency.

After the election, Hoover would go as far as to suggest that he sought Roosevelt's help because he believed that Roosevelt's very election and his economic plan—the New Deal—caused the panic.[20] The banking crisis, Hoover suggested, was a perceptual one, caused by the people's crisis of confidence in the president-elect. Consequently, withdrawing deposits in gold and currency were the result of fear of impending economic disaster. It probably escaped Hoover that he diagnosed the economic crisis as a perceptual one and thus rhetorical yet could not conceive a solution consistent with the diagnosis. Hoover lacked the ability to "appeal to sentiments of hope; neither his temperament nor his rhetorical talents were up to the task."[21] It was left for Roosevelt to take the rhetorical approach, and this he did on a grand scale.

Indeed, the lack of cooperation between the president and president-elect had its roots in Hoover's misperception of Roosevelt. Hoover developed a low regard for Roosevelt's capacity to govern and opined that the Democratic candidate for the presidency lacked the physical vigor to endure the campaign and the pressure of governing. This low regard for Roosevelt is well displayed in Hoover's initial reaction to Roosevelt's candidacy, which he welcomed with the comment that the New York governor was a lightweight given his bout with poliomyelitis and resulting physical limitations.[22] Once he realized his mistake and saw Roosevelt's strength, Hoover was concerned that Roosevelt's New Deal would change the entire American system, specifically "fifty years of progress toward individualism."[23] Consequently, Hoover opted to fight for his perspective in an effort to vindicate his administration's economic policies.

Hoover was not alone in his conviction that the Republican administration had the best approach to handling the economic crisis. His secretary of the treasury, Ogden Mills, also argued that the Republican administration was correct in its economic policies. This perspective was evident when Mills wrote on November 1932 two identical and confidential letters, one to Owen D. Young of General Electric, who was considered a candidate for treasury secretary in the incoming administration, and the second to George L. Harrison, governor of the New York Federal Reserve Bank. In the letter Mills wrote, "I am anxious about the situation which seems to be developing." Specifically, Mills outlined Congress's unwillingness to reduce expenditure "or to provide the necessary revenues to bring the budget into balance. They seem to be still living in a little world of their own without genuine realization of the gravity of the fiscal problem and its relationship to the general economic situation."[24] The problem, according to Mills, was the budget deficit and the Democrats' unwillingness to reduce it. The real concern, then, was with the New Deal, the expenditures it would bring, and the significantly changing role of government in the nation's economic life.

In a statement that would prove quite telling, Mills also wrote that, "if I were a dictator . . . the first two goals which I would reach for would be the balancing of the budget of the United States Government and the return of the gold standard by Great Britain."[25] In other words, given the Democratically leaning Congress and a Democratic president-elect waiting in the wings, the fear of an entirely new economic direction that could include inflationary measures, abandoning the gold standard, and consequently increasing the budget deficit could only be opposed with dictatorial measures. In a matter of weeks, Roosevelt would implement World War I legislation that gave him unprecedented powers to restore economic stability, a move that brought some to refer to him as a dictator.

It is possible that Hoover and Mills did not expect Roosevelt to issue statements that would be tantamount to giving up on his New Deal—that is, it is possible that the consistent pressure on Roosevelt during the interregnum was meant more for posterity and vindication of the Hoover administration and its economic policy and philosophy.[26] Roosevelt biographer Frank Freidel notes that for the defeated Hoover to ask president-elect Roosevelt to abandon his program in advance was quite an unusual move.[27] I am of the opinion that Hoover sought Roosevelt's help precisely because he held him in low regard and thus considered him weak and not principled enough to hold on to his New Deal vision.

Roosevelt, well coached by Moley, refused to issue statements despite Hoover's repeated urging. The principal argument Roosevelt used throughout the interregnum was that he had no official power or authority to issue any statement and that Herbert Hoover was the president. In one letter to Hoover, dated February 19, 1933, a letter that must have infuriated the president, Roosevelt stated:

> I am equally concerned with you in regard to the gravity of the present banking situation—but my thought is that it is so very deep-seated that the fire is bound to spread in spite of anything that is done by way of mere statements. The real trouble is that on present values very few financial institutions anywhere in the country are actually able to pay off their deposits in full, and the knowledge of this fact is widely held.[28]

At this phase Roosevelt was not keen on proposing rhetorical measures to calm the growing banking crisis. On the contrary, the crisis at hand, metaphorically depicted as an uncontrolled fire, had a life of its own, and the situation would get worse before it could get better. Roosevelt also stated that the banks' inability to pay was widely held knowledge. In other words, the Hoover administration had lost credibility over the banking crisis, and attempts to quiet the markets or insist that the banks were solvent would fail. Roosevelt gave Hoover a rhetorical explanation of why the crisis would spread, yet he argued that it was too late for Hoover respond rhetorically. The rhetorical act would be Roosevelt's. This would be precisely what Roosevelt planned to do—let the banking crisis intensify so that, by the time he assumed office, he could use the very severity of the crisis as the justification for its solution. Roosevelt would employ the rhetorical route only after assuming office. Perhaps deviously, he tried to dissuade Hoover from getting rhetorical so that he could take full advantage of a skill he knew he could master.

The exchange of letters and telegrams between Hoover and Roosevelt, as well as their meetings during the winter of 1932–33, must also be understood in a larger context of two different political philosophies, two distinct leadership styles and their differing rhetorical extensions. Hoover, the Great Engineer, was essentially a technocrat looking at issues from a technical perspective and seeking purely economic measures. As a conservative, he subscribed to the ideology of less government interference in the economy. Roosevelt, who by 1931 was calling on government to actively protect its citizens from disaster, emphasized moral leadership and a progressive philosophy.[29]

With Hoover's inability to get Roosevelt to cooperate, he sought another venue through his treasury secretary. On February 22, 1933, Hoover wrote Mills a "personal" memo about the secretary's upcoming meeting with the incoming treasury secretary, Woodin:

> I would be glad if you would assure him also that I join in a desire to cooperate in every possible way. The causes of this sudden critical development are simple enough. The public is filled with fear and apprehension over the policies of the new Administration.

People are acting now in individual self-protection, and unless it is checked, it jeopardizes every bank deposit, every saving, every insurance policy, and the very ability of the Federal Government to pay its way. The indices of fear are hoarding and flight of capital. The drain of gold is not yet alarming, yet its wide spread is symptomatic. The hoarding of currency however has risen to enormous dimensions and cannot go on at this rate without creating panic.[30]

And, continued Hoover,

The policies of which the public are mainly alarmed are first, inflation of the currency; second, failure to balance the budget; third, prospective projects which will overtax the borrowing power of the Government. These may or may not be the policies of the new Administration, but the actions of the majority party in Congress, the measures proposed by its members, and the failure of the President-elect to disavow them, and constant assurance of reversal of administration policies serve to confirm such public beliefs. The people do not wait to see these new policies developed after the administration comes into power. They are acting in self-protection before March 4th.

The way to stem the tide is that assurances should at once be given by the new administration that they rigidly oppose such policies. They alone can execute their assurances. That is the only way to reestablish confidence.

Hoover closed his memo by telling Mills, "I trust Mr. Woodin will realize that because a Republican Administration has stood staunchly for these principles and policies, it is no reason for their abandonment, for they are fundamental."

Hoover could not see beyond the paradigm in which he operated. He was utterly convinced that his diagnosis of the causes of the economic panic was correct and that his policies were fundamentally correct. It is fascinating to see the degree to which Hoover was correct about the public psychology of fear yet so incapable of figuring out how to deal with this phenomenon. The only solution Hoover would consider was for Roosevelt to go rhetorical—to issue statements, but only those that would accord with the Republican administration. In other words, Roosevelt should take on the rhetorical mantle and restore confidence to the economic markets. Hoover's conviction that the only way to solve the growing panic was for Roosevelt to abandon his economic agenda is most naïve and condescending. The letter carries a heavy dose of arrogance and a clear lack of respect for the president-elect and his policies.

Hoover was not done. On March 1, 1933, he sent Secretary Mills another memo, again suggesting that he tell Woodin of the administration's willingness for full cooperation but only if the president-elect agreed to a "line of sensible action which will meet the present banking situation." Hoover also suggested that it was his understanding that Congress would not act unless Roosevelt gave the legislative body his approval. Hoover closed his letter with a warning that "in view of our repeated offers to cooperate this very fact assesses him with responsibilities for the present situation which no amount of declamation can postpone until after March 4th."[31] In short, Roosevelt, who according to Hoover was not sensible, would be found responsible for the not helping solve the banking crisis.

It is rather clear in these two letters from the final days of the Hoover administration that Hoover was engaged in taking cover, seeking to secure a better historical record with regard to the banking crisis and the financial fiasco of the past few months. He would take no responsibility for anything; Roosevelt would bear all the responsibility for the economic fiasco, primarily for not telling a Democratic Congress what to do. Indeed, in a memo (it is unclear to whom it was sent, if it was sent at all), Hoover stated "that the governor's moral responsibility during the last two months rested on the fact that there was a Democratic House of Representatives which would take no action without his approval that he had intervened at one time to veto an agreement we had reached for balancing the budget and this established the fact that no legislation could take place without his approval."[32]

What is clearly missing from Hoover's agenda is an ability to articulate a rhetorical solution to the banking crisis. Hoover could go as far as understanding the vicious nature of fear that engulfed most bank depositors but could not go beyond technical measures to restore the needed confidence. Roosevelt, on the hand, would rely on the technical advice of Hoover holdovers but take the rhetorical perspective as key to restoring confidence to the markets.

When business activity slowed significantly in fall and winter of 1932–33, with some ten million unemployed, Roosevelt promised direct federal intervention to restore economic viability. His action-oriented New Deal advocated, albeit in great generalities, a new farm program, new public works, federal development, and regulation of power resources.[33] Despite the growing banking crisis, Roosevelt displayed no apprehension or concern. On the contrary, he appeared confident and optimistic. One could speculate that Roosevelt became even more optimistic and confident despite the worsening economic situation once he survived the assassin's bullet in Miami only seventeen days before inauguration. On that fateful day, February 15, Roosevelt displayed extraordinary courage as he refused the Secret Service directive to be driven out of harm's way, insisting instead on taking care of the one person seriously injured in the assassination attempt, Anton Cermak, the mayor of Chicago. Roosevelt personally held Cermak, checked his pulse, and calmed him as they drove to a nearby hospital.[34] Cermak would die about two weeks later, but Roosevelt, who came very close to being shot, may have seen himself as destined to preside over a national recovery.

The Run on the Banks

No single event caused the banking crisis in the winter of 1933, nor was there a sharp distinction between the banking crisis and the larger economic crisis since the stock market crash of 1929. For two years, bank failures flared up in various parts of the country, causing an overall sense of gloom and fear. The causes and effects of the intensification of the banking crisis were largely perceptual and may have been precipitated by several developments. Numerous bank failures led to an overall perception of financial volatility and fear of bank soundness. Beginning in November 1932, there were fears, both home and abroad, that the incoming Roosevelt administration would take the United States off the gold standard and through inflationary measures devalue the dollar.[1] Thus began a run on the banks and the depletion of gold and hard currency.[2] Though Roosevelt kept quiet on this issue, his plan all along was indeed to get the United States off the gold standard. Such a move would result in the devaluation of the dollar to a level more competitive with those of other trading nations. When foreign governments began to withdraw gold from the United States, fear of unsound banks quickly spread.[3] Another factor was the decision by Democratic leaders in Congress to publicize all loans to various banks made by the RFC.[4] This move to publicize which banks received federal loans, some four thousand in total, was a rhetorical blunder that made many depositors jittery about their bank accounts and brought many to withdraw their deposits. The bank failure was an added setback to an already desperate situation, with farm prices declining further since the summer of 1932, factory productivity slowing down, and unemployment increasing by about one million to a record of five million unemployed.[5]

Events leading to the State of Michigan declaring a bank holiday were most dramatic and revealing of an administration trying its best but being unable to salvage the banking crisis after it lost all credibility on economic issues. When the situation in Detroit began to deteriorate, Hoover sent Secretary of Commerce Roy D. Chapin and Undersecretary of the Treasury Arthur A. Ballantine to Detroit on February 13 to confer with Henry Ford, the one individual whose auto company had the funds to keep the banks afloat.

Their specific objective was to ask the Ford Company for a $7.5 million loan to the Detroit Union Guardian Trust Company, since the loans already extended to the banks by the RFC were insufficient. Henry Ford was antagonistic throughout the meeting. Ballantine outlined the bank's liabilities against depositors' demands and against loans already granted by the RFC. Without Ford's infusion of money, the two Hoover officials stated, "the Guardian banks would be forced to close. . . . The consequences of this would be to throw great pressure upon the First National Bank . . . group and upon all of the other banks in Michigan and . . . the consequences of that pressure would probably very soon extend outside of the State." Ford was unwilling to change his mind and at one point reiterated a statement made by Michigan senator Couzens, who, Ford said, "was probably right in saying 'Let the crash come.'"[6]

Later in the day Senator Couzens asked Ford to go along with the plan outlined by the administration. Ford not only refused but also threatened to withdraw his money from two national banks if the Guardian Trust Company did not open the next day. To preempt Ford's threat, F. Gloyd Awalt, acting comptroller of the currency, recommended closing both Detroit banks before Ford could implement his threat. Indeed, based on Awalt's recommendation, on February 14 Governor William A. Comstock declared a bank holiday for Michigan.[7]

This meeting between top Treasury and Commerce officials and Henry Ford underscored the difficult situation the Hoover administration faced in its inability to stop the deteriorating spiral of events. Upon leaving the meeting with Ford, Chapin and Ballantine noted that many banks "over wide areas . . . might have to go on a clearing house certificate basis."[8] This development added to the growing concern in the White House that actions were needed quickly and that, absent quick actions, a general banking crisis was imminent. And indeed such a crisis was already under way. After three years of the Depression, the notion that now the banking system would collapse as well was too much for many people, who sought to salvage whatever was left of their bank accounts. "Americans reacted this time with hair-trigger haste and last-ditch desperation. By the thousands, in every village and metropolis, they scurried to their banks, queued up with bags and satchels and carted away their deposits in currency and gold. They hoarded these precious remnants of their life savings under the mattress or in coffee tins buried in the back yard. Wealthier depositors shipped gold out of the country."[9]

On February 18, 1933, Hoover sent a ten-page handwritten letter to "President Elect Roosvelt," misspelling his name. In it, Hoover, displaying a keen appreciation for the rhetorical in economic behavior, explained the severity of the banking situation, describing it as "most critical" and noting that "the major difficulty is the state of public mind, for there is a steadily degenerating confidence in the future which has reached the height of general alarm. I am convinced that a very early statement by you upon two or three policies of your Administration would serve greatly to restore confidence and cause a resumption of the march of recovery."[10] In the same letter, Hoover argued that the recovery from the Depression began in the summer of 1932, and that the country had slipped back into an economic crisis during the winter of 1933. The blame, opined Hoover, fell squarely on Roosevelt's shoulders for refusing to commit to a conservative course of action.

As in the previous few months, Hoover asked Roosevelt to issue statements that would ensure no "tampering or inflation of the currency; that the budget will be unquestionably balanced, even if further taxation is necessary; that the Government credit will be maintained by refusal to exhaust it in the issue of securities."[11] It is unlikely that Hoover expected Roosevelt to accept his suggestions, which again implied abandoning the New Deal program. If Hoover sought to persuade Roosevelt to help the situation, accusing the president-elect of causing the banking crisis was a strange way to achieve this objective. The letter again displayed the low esteem Hoover held for Roosevelt and the degree to which he misunderstood him. Hoover said as much in a letter to Senator David Reed on February 20, 1933: "If these declarations be made by the President-elect, he will have ratified the whole program of the Republican administration: that is, it means abandonment of 90% of the so-called new deal."[12] Historian Hamby claims that Hoover was sincere in his letter to Senator Reed and that his statement must be read as the result of fear for the nation's economy.[13] Roosevelt, however, kept silent.

The run on the banks intensified in late February, with quantities of gold and currency being pulled out of U.S. banks at unprecedented levels. The Federal Reserve in New York saw its gold reserves reaching the dangerously low level of nearly 22 percent.[14] On February 24, 1933, William Woodin, the treasury secretary designate, was clearly worried over the run on the banks. That day, the banks in Baltimore collapsed and the governor of Maryland issued a three-day bank holiday. The following day, Roosevelt sent a laconic statement telling reporters that "he was studying the banking problems."[15]

On February 27, 1933, and likely with Hoover's urging, the New York Times called on Roosevelt to issue a statement necessary for averting a further run on the banks. Pressure was also mounting from European capitals to do something. Roosevelt, however, refused to issue specific comments. Instead he sent Woodin, who was invited by President Hoover and Secretary Mills for consultation "to learn the situation and to sit in on the various steps that were being taken."[16]

One Republican who was able to reach the president-elect was Thomas Lamont of the Morgan Company, who put it to Roosevelt in a succinct way: only a statement by the president-elect "could save the country from disaster." Lamont wanted Roosevelt to influence Congress to agree to specific measures that could save the situation: resumption of Federal Reserve purchases of unlimited government securities; RFC deposits of funds into weak banks without the need for securities; and the government raising $1 billion by March 15. Roosevelt issued only a vague statement through the press that he would cut the federal budget by 25 percent and that he would balance the budget. This statement was sufficient for many large banks but not for many small depositors who were worried about the safety of their small banks. Thus, the crisis continued.[17]

Despite this alarming development in the banking sector, Wall Street did not consider the crisis serious enough that it could spread nationwide. Roosevelt was also quite confident that the economic situation would improve once he assumed office, and he projected himself as such to his close advisers. During a lunch on February 25, 1933, with James H. Rand Jr. of Remington Rand, Rex Tugwell made an unfortunate statement to Rand, indicating that Roosevelt "was fully aware of the bank situation and that it would undoubtedly collapse in a few days, which would place the responsibility in the lap of President Hoover," and that the country would be rehabilitated after March 4. Rand quickly transmitted this conversation to Hoover, who used it to confirm that "Roosevelt and the New Dealers were disposed to bring the country to ruin for their own political ends."[18]

Hoover continued to send Roosevelt urgent messages, writing on March 1, 1933, that "I am confident that a declaration even now on the line I suggested . . . would save losses and hardships to millions of people."[19] At the final hours of the Hoover administration, the president continued to ask Roosevelt to commit to the policies of the outgoing Republican administration. Was Hoover resorting to sophisticated crisis rhetoric? Did he plan to use the crisis to force Roosevelt to change course, and did he threaten to blame the president-elect for the crisis if he would not cooperate? Hoover's message of March 1 and those preceding it do point in the direction of blaming the president-elect for the banking crisis.

The run on the banks worsened in the early days of March 1933, with some $226 million in gold reserves removed from banks (with more than $100 million in gold in domestic hoarding) and some $732 million in currency withdrawn as well. Yet, even now, the stock market continued to show resilience and trading was stable. The mood in the stock market was encouraging, and it was based on the assumption that confidence would be restored within days after Roosevelt's inauguration.[20] Roosevelt followed the stock market's confident activities as the best sign yet that he could end the run on the banks. This very optimism would explain much in Roosevelt's rhetoric during his first week in office, and especially in the approach he would take in his First Fireside Chat.

Trading with the Enemy Act of 1917: Hoover's Experience

When Roosevelt arrived in the nation's capital on March 2, 1933, he was informed that Hoover wanted to meet again and ask him to support a limited banking holiday until Monday, March 6, on condition that Roosevelt would also call Congress into a special meeting that day. If Roosevelt agreed, Hoover was willing to have the "Federal Reserve Board . . . approve an emergency guarantee of bank deposits."[21] After consultation with his advisers, Roosevelt suggested that Hoover declare a moratorium on bank activities until Saturday, March 4, and that Roosevelt would take responsibility after being sworn in on the same day. Hoover rejected Roosevelt's response.[22]

What kind of a game was Hoover playing? His request of Roosevelt to support a limited bank holiday until March 6, two days into the next administration, is very instructive. Hoover was still seeking to dictate policy to the new administration, continuing to search for ways to have Roosevelt share in the blame for the banking crisis. Roosevelt kept insisting, as he did throughout the winter, that Hoover was the president until March 4, making a clear line of separation between the two administrations. Roosevelt probably understood the rhetorical game Hoover was playing, and just as Hoover wished to construct an image of an uncooperative Roosevelt, the president-elect planned to construct the image of a courageous and able leader who in a matter of a few quick strokes would restore confidence. In the battle over the rhetoric of blame, Roosevelt clearly had the upper hand.

Excerpts from the diaries of Charles S. Hamlin (member of the Federal Reserve Board) about deliberation in the Hoover administration shed interesting light on events unfolding on March 2. At 9:30 p.m., Hoover's inner circle deliberated the merit of closing the banks. At the meeting, Governor Meyer informed the Federal Reserve Board that "the Attorney General had authorized Messrs. Harlan and Wyatt to tell the Secretary of the Treasury that there is sufficient color of authority under Trading with the Enemy Act to justify the President in taking action under it if he felt that the emergency justified it" (this practically meant declaring a bank holiday), and that the president could act under the emergency legislation "if he deemed the emergency great enough," but that "the matter was not free from doubt and he did not feel that he should advise the President to do so without the consent and approval of the incoming administration."[23] Awalt, in a memo of March 3, reporting about the same meeting, stated that the attorney general advised Hoover against using the war act to close the banks unless Roosevelt "agreed whole-heartedly and was willing to call [on Congress for] an extra session," and that "the authority under the Trading with the Enemy Act was very slim. In fact, the expression he used was that he had to go on a shoe string, but in the emergency he was willing to do so provided there was unanimous consent. Otherwise, he felt that the President was exceeding his powers and might even be impeached."[24] That the attorney general would be concerned with the president's impeachment during his final day in office is most puzzling legal advice.

Secretary Mills and Governor Meyer supported the use of the 1917 act to declare a banking holiday especially given the fact that "banks throughout the country were for all practical purposes closed, and that the drain on the remaining open institutions would probably be disastrous."[25] Upon receiving this report, the Federal Reserve Board unanimously felt that a banking holiday should be declared for Friday, Saturday, and Monday (March 3, 4, and 6, 1933) on the understanding that Congress would be called in for a special session to enact appropriate legislation. The Board then recommended to Hoover that he issue a proclamation closing all the banks in order to prevent a banking collapse. Wyatt took the opinion of Hoover's attorney general as vague enough for him to continue to press the White House to use the Trading with Enemy Act to close the banks, but treasury secretary Mills took a more cautionary tone in interpreting the attorney general's opinion. Governor Meyer, realizing Hoover's hesitancy, put it succinctly: "The question of legal authority is one thing and the question whether you will act with or without agreement with the President-elect is another thing."[26] Hoover's hesitancy continued and no action was taken.

Awalt's account of events after failing to reach Hoover on March 4 at 2 a.m. has Mills telling the late-night meeting of the Federal Reserve Board that there "was no chance of Mr. Hoover declaring a national holiday and the only thing left was for the governors of the states where Federal Reserve Banks were located to be persuaded to declare holidays."[27] Indeed, March 3, a day Awalt would refer to as the "day of the gold rush," brought the nation to the brink of financial collapse. "This run on gold was so desperate," added Awalt, "that it looked like something had to be done in New York."[28] On that day, the Federal Reserve Bank of New York lost over $200 million in gold and about $150 million in currency. This bank was now short some $250 million in reserves. The Federal Bank of Chicago was suffering similar withdrawals.[29]

With the banking crisis quickly reaching the level of panic, Hoover sought to use the customary visit to the White House by the president-elect on the eve of inauguration as one last opportunity to bring Roosevelt to do something.[30] When Roosevelt arrived at the White House on March 3, chief usher Ike Hoover (not a relative of the president) whispered to him that several Treasury officials would join. Roosevelt, feeling trapped, immediately summoned Moley. During the meeting, Hoover described the grim situation, said that "over a million dollars in gold has been withdrawn today, and the banks can't stand it," and asked Roosevelt to issue a statement regulating bank withdrawals.[31] Roosevelt, already irritated by the way Hoover had handled this customary meeting, replied that he would have to discuss this with his advisers and cut the meeting short.[32]

Hoover would try one last time. He called Roosevelt at 11:30 p.m. and asked that Roosevelt agree with him that there was no need to close the banks. Roosevelt told Hoover that he was with Senator Carter Glass and that the senator did not think that it was necessary to close all the banks and that the governors of each state could make that decision, as most already did. When the phone conversation ended, Senator Glass asked Roosevelt what he planned to do with the banks. To his astonishment, Roosevelt replied coyly, "Planning to close them, of course."[33]

Hoover finally gave up and went to bed for the last night in the White House. Moley left Roosevelt at 1 a.m. and headed to his room in the Mayflower for a few hours of sleep before the inauguration. However, in the lobby of the hotel he saw Woodin, who intimated to Moley that he could not fall asleep given the deteriorating banking crisis and asked him to walk with him to the Treasury office to see what help they could give. Roosevelt did not know of this visit, and years later Moley would write that he hoped the boss would not "repudiate our action."[34]

In the Treasury, Moley and Woodin found Mills, Meyer, and several others, all trying to find state governors to declare a bank holiday in their states. They spent the whole night convincing every governor to close the banks, thus legally making the bank closure a state action. The net effect of states closing their banks was that Roosevelt's proclamation of a banking holiday on March 6 was largely pro forma yet rhetorically a dramatic move with much symbolic importance. Thus, on the night of March 3 and the early morning of March 4, Hoover Treasury officials, with the help of Roosevelt's treasury secretary Woodin and adviser Moley, decided to close all the banks via the authority of state governors and thus began to put forward the initial plan to reopen sound banks.[35] They did so with Hoover's tacit approval, but in the final hours of the administration Hoover no longer mattered.

On the morning of Inauguration Day, March 4, Awalt was asked to attend a breakfast meeting with Secretary Mills in his office "to discuss the basis of some plan of approach to the problem of reopening the banks." The secretary of the treasury and several of his aides, only hours before the end of their administration's terms, were working hard to figure out the best plan for saving the banks. Awalt stated that "Mr. Mills was looking ahead," and that the participants in the meeting knew that the incoming president would have to issue a proclamation closing the banks. Mills focused on two important issues: identifying banks that could be reopened quickly, and figuring out how to keep them open.[36]

Thus commenced an interesting and critical collaboration between Hoover and Roosevelt officials. Roosevelt's key advisers, Moley and Woodin, would eventually join the Hoover Treasury officials—treasury secretary Mills, assistant treasury secretary Ballantine, acting comptroller of the currency Awalt, Federal Reserve Board researcher Dr. Emmanuel Goldenweiser, and legal counsel to the Federal Reserve Walter Wyatt—all trying to find a way out of the banking crisis.

Indeed, on March 4, Mills, Goldenweiser, and Awalt wrote Secretary Woodin a memorandum titled "Tentative Outline of a Possible Line of Approach to the Solution of our Banking Problem." The outline included the following items: a presidential proclamation to close all banks, the reopening of banks relative to their financial health, and classifying banks. Awalt estimated that about 2,200 banks, designated Class A, could be reopened quickly and be able to meet all demands. Banks that could not be reopened or needed major reorganization were designated Class C. All the rest of the banks were designated Class B. In a memo to incoming treasury secretary Woodin, Mills outlined the plan of action, suggesting the reopening of Class A banks as early as possible, supplying them with the necessary currency. After a brief interval "during which the public by experience would unquestionably find out that these banks were able to meet all demands, which would go a long way toward restoring confidence," banks belonging to Class B would be reopened as well.[37] Awalt did not believe Class C banks could be reopened, and if they could, it would be only after major reorganization.

In another account of events dated March 6, Awalt sheds additional light on the inner workings of the Hoover Treasury, two days after Roosevelt assumed office. On the afternoon of March 6, Mills asked Awalt to confer with him and others including Meyer, Harrison, and Wyatt. The meeting dealt with the plan to open as soon as possible some five thousand banks with 100 percent liquidity. The funds for these banks' liquidity would come from Federal Reserve loans. A debate ensued whether this measure of supplying funds for bank liquidity was deflationary or inflationary. Later in the day, the Hoover holdovers discovered that an entirely different plan had been adopted—one that in essence called for "opening of all the banks regardless of anything."[38] The crucial point here is that everyone was trying to figure out how to open the banks and which measures would be the most effective. That the ex-treasury secretary was meeting with holdovers to outline a plan for reopening the banks and to assess inflationary matters much despised by the Republican administration is rather ironic.

Not only did Hoover's key officials understand the measures necessary for inducing confidence into the banking system, they were also able to put forward the very plan that would alter the psychology of fear. They failed, however, to convince Hoover of the merit of their plans. Hoover hesitancy and concern over the legality of using the Trading with the Enemy Act to close the banks is difficult to understand. At this late juncture in his administration, any decisive action could only be seen as a necessary, even courageous, act and perhaps with time would vindicate his administration of earlier mistakes. In any event, any action Hoover would have taken was only a stopgap measure of about two days until the new administration took over, thus minimizing any major setback. Surely Hoover could have survived such a decisive action, especially if all he wanted was to vindicate his policies.

A Banking Holiday

Roosevelt was sworn in as president on Saturday, March 4, 1933. The inauguration day was constructed as a major rhetorical event, with Roosevelt addressing a distressed and fearful nation yearning for an end to the economic misery of the past three and a half years. Roosevelt framed his inaugural address around the perception of fear, indicating to the American people that the only thing they ought to fear was fear itself. In other words, he told people that there was no reason to fear anything since there was nothing material in the present situation that ought to have caused fear, except for unjustified fear. Hence, once people realized that they need not fear this unreasonable fear, they would stop fearing. The fear of the past few weeks, born out of the collapse of the nation's banking system and affecting its economic viability, was now described as "nameless, unreasoning, unjustified terror which paralyzes needed efforts to convert retreat into advance."[1] Roosevelt described the banking crisis as perceptual and not material, hoping that by framing the crisis this way he could also offer a quick solution in the form of confidence-building measures. He thus set the tone for his first week in office, replete with visible actions and accomplishments that collectively functioned rhetorically to impress the nation that their new leader's plan of action was serious and that it would yield the confidence the nation expected.

But why would Roosevelt cheapen the fear of losing life savings, bank deposits, life insurance, and basic monetary needs to run daily functions? And why would he suggest that there was no tangible fear in the current situation? Because Roosevelt subscribed to the notion that the banking crisis was brought about by a crisis of confidence, the result of panic that spread quickly despite the fact that a sufficient number of banks were solvent and stable. Roosevelt correctly assessed the situation as born out of the difficulties of a few insolvent banks and fear of their plight spreading throughout the nation. This fear brought panic, bank withdrawals, and the hoarding of gold, and soon thereafter banks began to collapse when they ran short on liquidity. In other words, a perceptual fear caused a tangible damage to many banks. Both Hoover and Roosevelt understood the psychological and rhetorical aspects of economic systems, but intuitively they differed on the merits of the rhetoric of economics.[2]

Was Roosevelt then engaged in transcendence, seeking now to suggest that there was no crisis at all? Not exactly. Though the crisis was brought on by fear, once bank withdrawals reached unprecedented low amounts of currency and gold reserves, it was difficult to restore confidence in the banking system, causing more banks to collapse. Roosevelt stated in his inaugural address that the "present situation" was serious and that such times require that we "speak the truth, the whole truth, frankly and boldly."[3] Franklin Roosevelt would speak frankly, suggesting that what was lacking in the present crisis was honest leadership, the kind that could restore confidence. Confidence then was the primary rhetorical commodity, and Roosevelt's leadership would restore it, implying that Hoover failed to use his leadership effectively.

Roosevelt would return to the theme of unjustified fear later in the address, this time stating that "our common difficulties . . . thank God, [are] only material things. . . . Our distress comes from no failure of substance," for the real culprits are "the unscrupulous money-changers," that is, bankers.[4] In other words, bankers were blinded by "mere monetary profit," not realizing the more important and noble social values. The falsity of "material wealth" is what Roosevelt wanted to correct, because it was the source of fear and the loss of confidence in the banking system. The scapegoats, then, were unscrupulous bankers and those who believed only in material wealth as distinct from spiritual wealth. Yet the restoration of confidence, Roosevelt stated, would come not from "changes in ethics alone. This nation is asking for action, and action now."[5] This call to action would be Roosevelt's central message. What likely eluded many was the realization that the actions Roosevelt called for were largely rhetorical—actions designed to project a dynamic and active administration, ready to restore the banking system and the nation's fiscal system back to a solid footing.

In other words, the crisis at hand was caused by a loss of confidence even though the crisis was not real but perceptual. Now, the crisis could be solved and must be solved only with real action as the means for the restoration of confidence. If this argument appears a non sequitur, it was. Roosevelt was correct that confidence had to be restored for banking to resume stability and solvency, and his description of the fear was rhetorically ingenious. This rhetorical formula allowed Roosevelt to suggest two ideas: One, despite all the difficulties of the banking crisis, the nation was strong and its resources plentiful, so fear should be replaced with hope and optimism. Two, despite the lack of material substance, once fear caused the run on the banks, only material (hence, substantive) action could restore confidence to the banking system. Most critical, the actions Roosevelt called for were fundamentally symbolic and thus rhetorical.

Thus, Roosevelt suggested that "this is no unsolvable problem if we face it wisely and courageously." He called for "strict supervision of all banking and credits and investments," an "end to speculation with other people's money," and a "provision for an adequate but sound currency." Together, these measures were described by Roosevelt as his "line of attack," to include calling Congress for a special session and outlining the measures for solving the banking crisis. The "attack" metaphor fit perfectly Roosevelt's call for action. And even though he initially stated that there was not much to fear but a psychological state of fear, there was much to fear and the fear was real when toward the end of the inaugural address Roosevelt described the nation as "stricken" and in the midst of a "national emergency" that required a "temporary departure from that normal balance of public procedure."[6] This contradiction notwithstanding, the call for suspending normal public procedures would become clear in less than forty-eight hours.

On March 5, Moley, together with Secretary of the Treasury Woodin and Attorney General Homer Cummings, drafted the executive order closing the banks through Thursday, March 9.[7] The proclamation stated that "in the best interests of all bank depositors ... a period of respite be provided with a view to preventing further hoarding ... and permitting the application of appropriate measures to protect the interests of our people."[8]

Most banks, however, had been closed earlier by state governors, some for several days and others for several weeks. On the same day, March 5, Roosevelt also met the nation's governors. The meeting was arranged weeks earlier, but given the banking crisis, Roosevelt would devote only five minutes to the governors. His remarks were rather general:

> We want if possible to have a general banking situation, that is to say, one covering national banks and State banks, as uniform as possible throughout the country. At the same time we want to cooperate with all the States in bringing about uniformity. I have no desire to have this matter centralized down here in Washington any more than we can help. I don't believe there is much more to say about banking.[9]

This brief statement must have been taken well by the nation's governors, whose primary interest was to maintain their authority over their states and against a federal supervisory role. Roosevelt provided noncommittal assurances that he was not interested in a centralized supervisory role for the federal government. But he did not rule it out. His message emphasized an active approach to solving the banking crisis, and the meeting only a day after his inauguration was part of the overall rhetorical plan to impress everyone with an active administration, taking charge of the crisis.

Late at night on March 5, Roosevelt called Wyatt to the White House prior to signing the proclamation closing the banks. Wyatt initially drafted the first version of the banking proclamation in January 1933, just in case Hoover requested it. However, by the time he went over it with Roosevelt, the proclamation had gone through several revisions. Now Roosevelt wanted Wyatt to review the proclamation with him one last time. Wyatt was the first to arrive at the White House, and Roosevelt asked him to read the proclamation and make any necessary suggestions. Wyatt read it and told Roosevelt that it was very similar to the one he drafted in January or February, and that the only modification he would now suggest was related to the issuance of scrip and restrictions on gold payment. Years later Wyatt would reflect that Roosevelt "seemed to understand the thing thoroughly."[10]

When Roosevelt was ready to sign the proclamation, closing all banks, the time was close to midnight on Sunday, March 5, 1933. Wyatt, now in the presence of several other close advisers, told the president:

> It's not very long till midnight. Your inaugural speech yesterday ended on a very deeply religious note, and I think impressed a great many people. The effect of that might be impaired if you sign this very important document on a Sunday. If you wait just a little while, you can sign it on a Monday. It won't make any practical difference, because we've got the thing all ready, we've got the telegrams all drawn, going to notify all Federal Reserve banks and 25 branches simultaneously by wire the minute you release it. So a short delay won't make any difference.

But before Roosevelt could react, someone in the room shouted, "Sign it and get it over, it won't make any difference." Roosevelt, the master of timing, replied, "Wyatt is right," and waited until after midnight, thus affixing the date of Monday, March 6, on the proclamation.[11]

Trading with the Enemy Act of 1917: Roosevelt's Experience

Using a war statute as justification for closing all banks was legally weak. Both Hoover and Roosevelt knew this, but a different approach to the

Trading with the Enemy Act of 1917 made all the difference between Hoover's failure and Roosevelt's success.

Unlike Hoover, Roosevelt was not concerned with the legal precedent used to justify closing the banks. Wyatt told Roosevelt that he had the right to close the banks even though "Hoover's Attorney General doubted it very much."[12] Although Hoover's chief legal adviser was inclined not to support using the 1917 act, Roosevelt's attorney general, Homer Cummings, issued a quick ruling, giving the president the green light to use this act.[13]

The Trading with the Enemy Act, which initially was limited to transfers of gold, silver, and currency, was now interpreted to cover also the transfers of credit that accounted for about 90 percent of all business transactions.[14] The act stated that "the President may investigate, regulate, or prohibit, under such rules and regulations as he may prescribe, by means of licenses or otherwise, any transactions in foreign exchange, and the export, hoarding, melting, or earmarking of gold or silver coin or bullion or currency."[15] Clearly Hoover's Treasury officials had advocated a bank holiday and considered this law sufficient for its implementation, but Hoover was reluctant to use it. Years later, Hoover would criticize Roosevelt for doing the very thing his own Treasury officials advocated.

The proclamation closing the banks was justified, stated Roosevelt, by the "heavy and unwarranted withdrawals of gold and currency from our banking institutions for the purpose of hoarding." A "continuous and increasingly extensive speculative activity abroad in foreign exchange has resulted in severe drains on the Nation's stocks of gold," and these conditions "have created a national emergency." To prevent further hoarding of currency and gold, "it is in the best interests of all bank depositors that a period of respite be provided with a view of preventing further hoarding."[16]

The proclamation not only closed banks but also prohibited the hoarding or melting of coins and speculation in foreign exchange. It also stipulated steps to be taken in cases of violations. Finally, the proclamation outlined specific provisions for planning the reopening of banks, authorizing the secretary of the treasury to allow some banking institutions to perform limited function, to allow for the issuance of clearing house certificates, and to create special trust accounts to receive new deposits. This last item was an important step and a hint of things to come. These new accounts would be separated from old accounts subjected to limited withdrawal; they would be subject to withdrawal without restriction. Roosevelt used the proclamation to close the banks as politically necessary, but also rhetorically to impress the nation with his activism and determination and to convince the American people that a serious plan for reopening banks was under way.

Beyond the technicalities and legalities involved in closing the banks, the bank holiday brought the nation major difficulties of unprecedented proportion. The country's economy was severely disrupted as individuals, services, and industries ran out of currency, restricting many trade and commercial transactions and causing disruption to many economic and fiscal necessities usually taken for granted. While some ran out of coins, others found it difficult to exchange notes of $10 and more. Some industries and services printed their own temporary currency notes and IOU's; many others could not purchase basic essentials.

Roosevelt extended the bank holiday on March 9, declaring that "technical difficulties which operated to delay the opening of the banks ... have ... substantially been overcome by tireless work on the part of the officials of the Treasury and the Federal Reserve System," and that the banks would reopen on Monday, Tuesday, or Wednesday. Roosevelt also announced his intention to speak over the radio on Sunday, March 12, at 10 P.M.[17]

There were also hopeful signs. To alleviate some of the difficulties, the Treasury authorized some limited banking for the March 6–8 period. This modification in the banking holiday was possible because of an improvement in the nation's gold reserve since March 4. Since Inauguration Day, and due in part to the new administration's plan to list the names of those who withdrew gold since February 1, 1933, depositors began to bring money and gold back to their banks. The return of gold was significant enough that by Friday, March 10, some $300 million in gold had been recovered.[18]

To impress the nation that the new president was actively working to end the banking crisis, Roosevelt continued to engage in rhetorical acts. He met with his budget director, Lewis Douglas, to assess the budget deficit left by the Hoover administration and decided on major cuts in the budget. More important, Roosevelt also decided to publicize the deficit of $1,358,993,357 for the final days of the previous administration, as well as a deficit of $2,900,000,000 for the fiscal year (ending the previous June 30).[19] The idea was simple: blame the previous administration as much as possible. Recall that Hoover kept insisting that the budget deficit must be reduced. Now Roosevelt could point to the irresponsible budget deficit left by the previous administration and present his responsible plans for necessary cuts. This publicized act also implied that Hoover could have done the very thing Roosevelt was doing in his first week in office—reduce the budget deficit.

During the first week in office, and largely as part of Roosevelt's rhetorical package, he also conducted his first press conference, the likes of which journalists had not experienced. Whereas Hoover's relationship with the press was rather tense, Roosevelt invited the press for an informal exchange of questions and answers. On March 8, press representatives were in for a surprise when they attended a relaxed presidential press conference. The photographs of this event illustrate the informal, lively, and relaxed setting.[20] Roosevelt, seated, smiling, and surrounded by cheerful newspapermen, used this press conference to send a message of confidence to the nation.

He told the press that the government was initially thinking of issuing scrip as a means to provide adequate currency to failing banks, but "if things go along as we hope they will, the use of scrip can be very greatly curtailed, and the amounts of new Federal Bank issues, we hope, can be also limited to a very great extent."[21] The message was clear: Confidence was now based on actual positive developments; the banking situation was improving by the hour, making artificial measures such as scrip less necessary.

At the press conference Roosevelt was asked to define the phrase "adequate but sound" currency. He responded that he could not define adequate or sound currency "too closely one way or another." In expounding on the phrase, Roosevelt again sought to project optimism, stating that he was talking about "managed currency, the adequateness of which will depend on the conditions of the moments," and since conditions had already improved enough to rule out the need for scrip, the term must be flexible for efficient policy implantation. When pressed further to define "adequate," Roosevelt tersely replied, "I don't want to define 'sound' now. . . . The real mark of delineation between sound and unsound is when the Government starts to pay its bills by starting printing presses. That is about the size of it."[22] The ambiguity must be understood as Roosevelt's strategic approach to introducing a significant policy change—introducing inflationary measures as the strongest hint that he planned to take the United States off the gold standard.

Roosevelt also told the press that in his proposed legislation he would ask Congress "for fairly broad powers in regard to banking—such powers that would make it possible to meet the changing situation from day to day in different parts of the country. We cannot write a permanent banking act for the nation in three days." As he had done thus far and would continue to do throughout the volatile first week, Roosevelt appeared to let the crisis scene "dictate" policy and action, proposing measures necessitated by momentary circumstances. The public justification for closing the banks was now expanded to include general management of the banking crisis.[23]

The press conference illustrates just how crucial it was for Roosevelt to ensure that the press did not project unnecessary fear. When he was asked about the kind of guarantees the government was willing to issue in order to protect bank deposits, Roosevelt described, off the record, the difficulty the government had with the word "guarantee," illustrating this difficulty with the case of three different banks—one that could pay 100 percent of all depositors' demands, one that could pay only 50 percent, and one that could pay only 10 percent. If the government assumed 100 percent guarantees in these cases, explained Roosevelt, it would mean no losses to the government with the first bank, 50 percent losses to the government with the second bank, and 90 percent losses with the third. In other words, general guarantees would result in major losses to the government, a risk it could not and should not take.

Roosevelt hoped that this very honest and direct explanation would bring the press representatives to understand the importance of confidence-building press reports. The president was at times coy with the press, purposefully vague so as to not allow unnecessary attributions. Other times Roosevelt was more direct, hoping that an off-the-record and direct statement would be considered more credible. Roosevelt also sought to use privileged information to dissuade the press from the sensational and the provocative.

Thus, what Roosevelt said to the press, but only off the record, was that

> there are undoubtedly some banks that are not going to pay one hundred cents on the dollar. We all know it is better to have that loss taken than to jeopardize the credit of the United States Government further in debt. Therefore, the one objective is going to be to keep the loss in the individual banks down to a minimum, endeavoring to get 100 percent on them. We do not wish to make the United States Government liable for the mistakes and errors of individual banks, and put a premium on unsound banking in the future.[24]

The crisis at hand was about people's confidence in the banking system and in Roosevelt's ability to restore confidence. It is quite possible, just as Hoover suggested, that Roosevelt used the crisis as a tool for effective governing. He would let the crisis intensify, do nothing to help Hoover so that his decisive action would be seen as indicative of his exceptional leadership skills, thus allowing him to propose and implement significant, even radical changes in the economic and political systems. Roosevelt managed all of this while maintaining the appearance that he was skilled at reacting to the critical situation.

Roosevelt's overall objective was to present symbolically a dramatic turn of events since assuming office and significant changes in leadership and decision making relative to the previous administration.

Closing the banks, issuing statements on the budget deficit, and the press conference were visual and symbolic representations of significant changes undertaken by Roosevelt. Collectively, these changes functioned to present Roosevelt's entry into the White House as refreshing and projecting leadership skills the country needed to solve the crisis Hoover left behind.

The rhetorical in Roosevelt's dramatic decision to close the banks is aptly described by historian James MacGregor Burns: "Roosevelt played his role of crisis leader with such extraordinary skill that his action in *keeping* the banks closed in itself struck the country with the bracing effect of a March wind."[25]

CHAPTER 5

Crafting the Emergency Banking Act

The banking crisis could not be solved without the legislation necessary to authorize emergency measures. Roosevelt's efforts were directed toward this important legislation and quick enactment of the Emergency Banking Act. The most significant development in getting the act drafted and implemented was the work of several Hoover holdovers, all Treasury officials who stayed over and continued in their previous positions. The key individuals the Roosevelt administration asked to stay were Arthur A. Ballantine, undersecretary of the treasury, F. Gloyd Awalt, acting comptroller of currency, and Walter Wyatt, researcher of the Federal Reserve Board.

In the view of the outgoing Treasury officials, "the incoming administration apparently had no plans about the banking system, none whatever. I don't know what the devil would have happened if there hadn't been a small group of devoted people there in the Treasury Building."[1] Though one is tempted to take such self-assessment with a grain of salt, there is truth to this assertion in the sense that the expertise of managing the banking crisis was clearly in the hands of Hoover's Treasury officials. It would be erroneous, however, to conclude that Roosevelt was unaware of the banking crisis. If anything, he understood the banking crisis perfectly well. What is most important is that, despite the pressures of the first few days in office, Roosevelt possessed the political leadership and rhetorical skills to bring the banking crisis to a successful end. Roosevelt also trusted his close aides to bring him a workable plan to reopen the banks.

Moley and Woodin met on Monday, March 6, to assess the banking situation. Writing several years later, and no longer a fan of Roosevelt, Moley stated that the president was so busy with other matters that he had "only the sketchiest notions of what remained to be done." He and Woodin concluded that action taken must "swiftly [be] put in effect." But how would the public react? "We knew," wrote Moley, "how much of banking depended upon make-believe or, stated more conservatively, the vital part that public confidence had in assuring solvency." Therefore, only "swift and decisive and well-publicized action by Roosevelt and Congress" would restore confidence.[2] Moley, who had worked on Roosevelt's inaugural address for several months, was the closest person to appreciate his rhetorical proclivities and his penchant for drama in politics. An emphasis on swift action would be quite in line with the boss's way of doing things.

Moley claims that he and Woodin planned to suggest to Roosevelt that he "should announce the plans to the press on the Saturday following and to the people on Sunday night on the radio networks. There was magic, we knew, in that calm voice." With a plan to reopen the banks under way, Woodin, Moley, Ballantine, and George W. Davidson, the president of the Hanover Bank in New York, met with Roosevelt and presented him the plan.[3] The plan, presented to Roosevelt on March 6, was based on a plan drafted by Mills, Goldenweiser, and Awalt, all Hoover's Treasury officials on March 4 and included the following outline:[4]

Solvent banks, as authorized by the Federal Reserve System, would open on Friday, March 10.

Banks not part of the Federal Reserve System would open as well, provided the Treasury was assured of their solvency.

Banks that were not wholly solvent must be reorganized first and be opened as soon as possible, and such banks in cities with populations of 100,000 and over should be dealt with first.

The Federal Reserve Banks would loan funds to banks, corporations, and individuals on notes secured by the government.

The Federal Reserve Banks would lend currency to any solvent
bank against sound assets, regardless of the bank's size.

The Federal Reserve Banks would issue Federal Reserve notes
against secured assets of any kind.

The embargo on gold and measures to prevent hoarding of gold
and currency would continue.

One modification to this plan was made by Woodin on March 7. As he
told Moley, he made several critical decisions regarding the banks:

> First, that there was going to have to be some kind of governmental
> control of banking. This would in no sense imply any taking over
> of the whole system, but merely centralized governmental regula-
> tion in the interest of the people. The second decision was against
> the issuance of scrip as advocated by many, and pro the issuance
> of additional Federal Reserve Bank notes, on the basis of sound
> assets of banks which heretofore had not been legally valid as bases
> for the issuance of such notes.[5]

These were critical decisions, for they simplified the process of reopening the banks and sent a clear signal that the banking situation had
begun to improve even before banks were reopened. Moley would later
praise Woodin for "bearing up beautifully" and for the "calm and stability of the man. He has really kept his head and was able to disregard
such advice as was thrown at him with terrific pressure."[6]

The critical decision, then, was to save the banks but not to reform
them, at least not now.[7] The crisis left no time for such a long-term
process; it required a quick restoration of confidence. Most significant,
this outline would be incorporated in Roosevelt's First Fireside Chat.

The outline also meant that only a few days after Roosevelt chastised
the "money-changers" for their greed and irresponsibility, the bankers
were essential for the quick resumption of normal banking operations.
One way to rationalize this about-face lies in understanding Roosevelt's

approach to the crisis and its solution as primarily conservative and partially rhetorical. Roosevelt relied on Hoover's Treasury officials and adopted the very policies they had developed for Hoover, who rejected them. The principal distinction between Hoover and Roosevelt was that Hoover was hesitant and incapable of approving the needed plan, though his advisers knew much better than he what should be done. It is equally likely that, even if Hoover did implement the advice his Treasury suggested, the situation would not have improved, because the crisis needed a new face, a new leader with rhetorical skills Hoover could only dream of. The restoration of confidence could be only Roosevelt's, not Hoover's.

From the outset, the crisis would be seen from two complementary perspectives: a technical one, primarily in the hands of Hoover holdovers, and a rhetorical one, in the hands of Roosevelt and Moley. The rhetorical approach could not, however, have worked without the technical expertise. It is also important to understand what was not in the plan to reopen the banks: the plan did not carry a Republican or a Democratic platform; the plan was a practical one, designed for quick implementation. For this very reason, Roosevelt adopted the Hoover Treasury's plan.

Wyatt identifies Ballantine and Awalt as the officials who saved the day. Wyatt also opined that "poor, dear Mr. Will Woodin was a sweet man, but he didn't know the first thing about [the banking crisis]." In particular, Wyatt lauded Ballantine as the key figure in the banking drama and the one who functioned as the liaison between the Hoover Treasury and Roosevelt, the one who "saved the situation."[8] Ballantine would get the banking legislation drafted, have Roosevelt approve it, get it through Congress, and then draft the First Fireside Chat.

On Tuesday, March 7, at 10 P.M., Wyatt was called to the secretary of the treasury's office. In the office were present other officials including Secretary Woodin, Assistant Secretary Ballantine, George L. Harrison, Awalt, and Moley. Wyatt was told to take charge of drafting an emergency banking act. When he inquired into the details, he realized that "what they were talking about was what we had been discussing off and on since January and February 1933." The details of the act were complicated but, in essence, designed to help solvent and not so solvent banks reopen. If the comptroller found a bank to be insolvent, the comptroller would appoint a receiver to liquidate the bank's assets. In the meantime, depositors could not withdraw their money and the bank could make no loans. The appointment of a receiver meant the death of a bank. Short of this drastic action, the comptroller could try to save a bank by infusing capital in the form of cash deposits or newly issued stock. This option, however, was often not realistic, for hardly anyone would buy stock in an insolvent bank.[9]

The ideal was to find a way to suspend a bank's activities without appointing a receiver, hoping to reopen the bank at a later date. This option meant the appointment of a conservator, not a receiver, with the authority to replace existing management. The conservator had several measures available, including assessing the bank's assets to determine if depositors could withdraw 10 percent of their deposits, accepting new deposits, separating them from old deposits, and allowing their withdrawals of 100 percent.

These specific measures, which culminated in the Bank Conservation Act, were drafted by Wyatt in February 1933 and would be Roosevelt's path in formulating his emergency banking bill. Another bill Wyatt had drafted several weeks earlier would authorize the issuance of preferred stock by national banks and their purchase by the RFC. At the time of drafting this bill in January and February 1933, Wyatt was not allowed to keep a copy, since "somebody had thought it was dangerous," so he gave his only copy to Awalt, who locked it in his office safe. When Wyatt was asked to draft an emergency banking act, he asked Awalt to get that first stock bill out of his safe and he modified it.[10]

Roosevelt, leaving nothing to chance, asked the Senate and House leaders to meet with him on March 8 late at night and informed them of the emergency banking bill he would introduce to Congress the following day. When he finished his draft, Ballantine took it to Roosevelt. It was then modified following requests by Senator Glass. The draft was finalized around 3 A.M. on Thursday, March 9, when Ballantine and Wyatt went to the White House to discuss the final provisions with Roosevelt and Woodin. Wyatt reminisced that the proposed bill was so well received that he thought Woodin was going to kiss him.[11] When he left the White House in the early hours of March 9, Woodin was asked by a reporter if the emergency bill was finished, to which Woodin replied, "Yes, it's finished. Both bills are finished. You know my name is Bill and I'm finished."[12]

Early March 9, Roosevelt informed the nation about the measures he had sent Congress, measures that "will immediately relieve the situation and at once start banking operations throughout the entire country. I have been assured that there is every prospect of the immediate passage of this legislation on its introduction. I am gratified at this outlook."[13] Roosevelt's short press statement is instructive. He used the word "immediate" twice; he talked about assurance, relief, and the reopening of the banks at once. Time was the master metaphor, for Roosevelt understood how anxious the people were; all they needed to hear was that action had been taken and that the situation would improve quickly.

Awalt's Master Text

On March 9, Roosevelt also sent a message to Congress as a preamble to his emergency banking proposal. The origin of this message is rhetorically important and can shed additional light on the strong collaboration between the Hoover Treasury holdovers and Roosevelt's rhetoric.

Among Awalt's papers deposited in the Herbert Hoover Presidential Library is an interesting text that carries neither a title nor an official date. A handwritten note on the top right margin reads as follows: "Statement prepared by Mills + issued by Woodin, March 8, 1933." Both archivist Craig Wright of the Hoover Library and I speculate that, given the fact that the text is part of Awalt's confidential papers and was prepared by him and not by Mills, it served as a master text from which Roosevelt and his aides could draw specific ideas. The text was written for Roosevelt most likely as a draft for the introduction accompanying the emergency banking proposal. This can be discerned from two declarations. One states, "Late Saturday evening I took such action under the authority granted by one of the War Statutes still in existence," a reference to the March 4 decision to use the Trading with the Enemy Act of 1917, which grounded Roosevelt's authority to close the banks and call for emergency legislation. A second statement outlined that "if the necessary legislation is enacted on Thursday a very great number of banks in all sections of the United States . . . can be opened on a 100 per cent basis," the very gist of Roosevelt's plan to reopen the banks.[14]

Several portions of this text found their way into Roosevelt's message to Congress accompanying his banking proposal, and others appeared in the First Fireside Chat. The text is intriguing in that it appears to have been written with Roosevelt's character and rhetorical proclivities in mind, a fit Awalt accomplished in a rather short time since Inauguration Day. The very first sentence in the text—"By Saturday evening of last week practically all of the banks throughout the United States had ceased to perform normal banking functions"—would appear in the message to Congress with only slight modification but with a clearer punch: "On March 3, banking operations in the United States ceased."[15]

In Awalt's draft the banking crisis "grew out of a variety of causes which, for present purpose, it is unnecessary to analyze. The central factor, however, which must be grasped in order to develop a remedy is that the crisis is basically a banking crisis, and only in a secondary degree a currency crisis." Roosevelt's message to Congress would again be truncated and pointed: "To review at this time the causes of this failure of our banking system is unnecessary. Suffice it to say that the Government has been compelled to step in for the protection of depositors and the business of the nation."[16] Again Roosevelt favored the shorthand and the direct appeal, but he made a significant change to Awalt's sentence. In Awalt's draft, the crisis at hand is defined, thus implying some governmental responsibility. Roosevelt, consistent with his rhetoric thus far, took the scenic imperative whereby the crisis occurred outside the purview of the government. With this approach, Roosevelt's version continued to present the new administration as the nation's savior, taking the necessary measures to help the nation. The banking crisis, then, was not Roosevelt's fault but his responsibility to the American people nonetheless. Consequently, much of the people's respect and support for their president rested in their appreciation of his skilled approach to a banking crisis he inherited.

The rhetorical insights to be drawn from this text about fear and confidence in the context of the banking crisis are intriguing. Awalt writes that "as a result of the unprecedented number of bank failures during the course of the last few years, the confidence of the people has been shaken, and without confidence no banking system can function adequately," and that "with fear feeding on fear the process of attrition and dissipation of our banking resources through hoarding grew at a constantly accelerated pace."[17] Awalt understood perfectly Roosevelt's inaugural call "to fear fear" and modified this double take with "fear feeding fear." Awalt was also familiar with his previous boss, President Hoover, and his repeated references to the need to restore people's confidence as essential to a healthy economy. That Awalt opted for the more Rooseveltian phrasing and the emphasis on fear shows how quickly the new president's rhetorical impact had been felt, even by Hoover's holdovers.

Awalt's draft puts great emphasis on the need to act in a timely fashion: "In the present circumstances the time element is all-important. By the end of the week we must have banks open throughout the United States. They must be sound banks. They must command the full confidence of the people." Roosevelt again would cut to the chase, stating: "Our first task is to reopen all sound banks. This is an essential preliminary to subsequent legislation directed against speculation with the funds of depositors and other violations of positions of trust."[18] Here Roosevelt showed his superb rhetorical skills. The need to reopen banks quickly was clear, but he altered Awalt's reference to confidence by hitting again on the culprits, just as he did in his inaugural address. Roosevelt understood his audience—Congress as the embodiment of the people—and he understood the need to indicate to Congress that this president understood who was responsible for the banking crisis and the overall economic emergency. In any event, persuasion is often more successful when it identifies culprits.

Awalt would see one point in his text find its way to the First Fireside Chat. He writes: "It should be clearly understood . . . that if a bank does not reopen at once on a 100 per cent basis it does not in any sense carry with it the implication that such a bank is unsound. It simply means that either its officers and directors have not felt ready as yet to reopen fully, or that the official authorities have not found time to pass upon its application."[19] This phrasing would be ideal for Roosevelt, who had to develop a speech that would remove as much as possible any lingering suspicion that some unopened banks were not sound or that perhaps they were on the verge of collapse. Awalt supplied a technical justification that would do wonders to restore people's confidence once banks reopened, albeit at a gradual rate.

The individual most responsible for drafting the First Fireside Chat is Arthur Ballantine. Given the affixed date of March 8 on Awalt's untitled text, the only logical explanation for Awalt's text being used for at least two rhetorical outlets is that Awalt and Ballantine, the two top Hoover holdovers, worked closely together. Throughout the final days of the Hoover administration, and especially during the first week of Roosevelt's administration, Ballantine and Awalt worked jointly on several projects, with Ballantine organizing all major initiatives including the proclamation closing the banks, the message to Congress, the emergency banking bill, and the First Fireside Chat.

It must be recognized that the banking crisis operated in the context of great concern over further bank failures. The Treasury in particular was concerned that, if only a few solvent banks reopened, this would be tantamount to proof that the fear over the soundness of banks was justified, leading to a great paralysis of the system. The consequences of the vast majority of people finding themselves unable to withdraw money for normal operations, and the nation's commerce and industry unable to resume operations, were detrimental to the continuation of the United States as an industrial power. Thus the plan to reopen the banks had to be taken as credible and convincing, so that any continued run on any bank would immediately cease once depositors realized that the panic was over.

In a memo dated March 6, 1933 (the memo does not state to whom it was addressed), Awalt addressed the concern over what would happen once the banks were reopened. He writes that in some locations where there are A banks, "depositors would have complete confidence in banks opened" when government assurances and Federal Reserve notes ensured solvency. Awalt was also convinced that large depositors would not be tempted to withdraw money and that "any run by small depositors would rapidly dry up when they found that their demands were promptly met."[20] The real concern was with communities without an A bank.

Awalt resorted to one example for relieving depositors' concerns, an example that could not be construed as naïve:

> Taking Detroit as an example, the Secretary of the Treasury, speaking for the President, would offer to establish a new bank, the Treasury to furnish the capital through the purchase of preferred stock in the First National Wayne Bank and the Guardian Commerce Bank to turn over the new bank certain of their assets in return for the assumption by the new bank of, say, 40 percent of their deposit liabilities. Public opinion would unquestionably compel the adoption of this program in their particular locality.[21]

Given the particular development surrounding the Guardian Bank and Henry Ford's refusal to help, a development that clearly exacerbated the general run on the banks, the use of Detroit as an example of a bank failure is revealing. Perhaps this example was a payback-in-kind to Ford for his refusal to help with the Detroit bank (see chapter 3). Ford's role notwithstanding, the Treasury was clearly creative in its plan for restoring public confidence in the banking system. Credibility of every bank's ability to handle all depositors' demands was the key to a successful end to the banking crisis.

Would the Emergency Banking Act bring the difficult winter months to an end? Would banks' solvency be restored? The proposed bill had to pass muster with congressional leaders and their banking committees. The work of Hoover's holdovers was again indispensable. When, upon Ballantine's insistence, the exhausted Wyatt went home to sleep, his rest was cut short once Senator Glass discovered that he was missing from the final consultation in his Senate office. "You get him out of bed," Glass told Ballantine, "and get him down here, nobody can explain this but him, and he's got to explain it to me, so I'll know what it's all about." At 2:00 o'clock in the morning of March 9, the executive meeting of the Senate Banking and Currency Committee met. After some additional modifications and more drafting, Senator Glass gave a copy of the emergency banking proposal to Henry Steagall, chairman of the House Banking and Currency Committee. Once Steagall had the copy in his hand, he entered the House chambers, already in session, stating, "Here is the bill, let's pass it." The bill passed in a short session with no other member of the House having a copy of the bill but Chairman Steagall.[22]

Passing the Emergency Banking Act in the Senate took a bit longer, with the Senate Banking and Currency Committee discussing it in detail. One of the remaining sticky issues was the number of national banks that could be opened without the act, and the number that could be opened with it. Awalt estimated that about 2,400 national banks could be opened without the act and that about 5,000 banks could be opened only with the Bank Conservation Act.[23]

At around 4:30 in the afternoon, the proposal was brought to the floor of the Senate. The ensuing debate took about two and a half hours. Only Louisiana Senator Huey Long engaged in demagoguery and opposed the bill on the Senate floor, arguing that it would needlessly hurt many little banks. Senator Glass argued that the root problem in the collapse of banks was the "little corner grocerymen who run banks"[24] and the "lack of proper supervision of them by state authority." The testy exchange lasted only a few minutes and ended with Senator Glass telling his colleague from Louisiana that he did not know what he was talking about. The Senate passed the banking bill 73 to 7.[25]

At 7 P.M., President Roosevelt signed the Emergency Banking Act. The passage of this bill in one day was unprecedented, but all participants understood the need for quick action. The legislation itself, as Wyatt would state years later, "stood the test of time."[26] The passage of the Emergency Banking Act was rhetorically significant in projecting an active administration and legislation that heeded the president's request for quick action. The restoration of confidence was under way, and the comparison with the inactivity of the Hoover administration could not be more profound. The very fact that both houses of Congress passed this important legislation in a matter of hours must have bothered Hoover a great deal. After all, he predicted all along that Roosevelt would have to take full responsibility for the banking crisis and that after March 4 it would become clear just how irresponsible Roosevelt was. This course of events did not materialize, and Hoover's sour grapes were clear in a phone conversation with Mills on March 10, 1933.

The phone exchange between Hoover and Mills illustrates how little Hoover understood Roosevelt's rhetorical skills. When Mills suggested that the banking bill "will work efficiently," Hoover replied that "it is going to raise the most appalling difficulties." When Mills suggested that, according to Awalt, about 6,800 banks would be in a position to reopen, with 5,000 to be opened at once, Hoover replied that the government would end up with preferred stock in some ten to twelve thousand state banks. Mills quickly retorted, "No; no state banks get this [preferred stock] unless it takes out a national charter." Hoover, however, opined that the banks could not get a subscription of preferred stock without a national charter. Mills again corrected Hoover, telling him that the banks must first take out a national charter. Hoover suggested that the plan to reopen banks would result in "some temporary inflation," and both Hoover and Mills predicted a disorderly reopening of banks, thus causing further harm to the banks. Yet, when Hoover suggested that the plan to reopen banks would result in a lot of political pressure to open even ten or twenty banks, Mills replied that this would not happen because the plan for the reopening of the banks was taken very seriously. Hoover would not relent. He suggested to Mills that the bill did not address small banks and that it was "really a big bank bill." Again Mills contradicted his old boss: "It really is not, Mr. President." Finally, when Hoover contemplated another banking failure, Mills replied, "I don't think so."[27]

It is easy to understand why Hoover would take a negative view of the banking situation, yet interesting to see Mills presenting an objective and even hopeful perspective. Did Hoover misunderstand the banking crisis altogether, or was he simply unwilling to see Roosevelt succeed? His opinion expressed in the phone conversation does suggest a limited understanding of the intricacies of the banking crisis and a disdain for Roosevelt for accomplishing much in a matter of days.

The efforts of officials from both the Hoover and Roosevelt Treasury to solve the banking crisis were commendable. While one is tempted to assume that Hoover and Mills would object to the assistance outgoing Treasury officials gave the Roosevelt administration, both were supportive of these efforts, in large part believing that the assistance of the holdovers and Hoover's policies would be vindicated after all. After Roosevelt assumed office, Mills would visit the Treasury during the first few days of the new administration. On one such visit, Wyatt heard Mills tell Ballantine (in reference to the Thomas Amendment in April 1933), "This is a terrible thing. Get some of the boys and bring them up to my house, and let's see if we can't have some argument against it." Ballantine replied, "Ogden, you don't know what you are asking me. I'm here trying to help Mr. Roosevelt. . . . I can't do that."[28] After that, Mills did not visit the Treasury again.

The Treasury holdovers were more than loyal to the new administration. During Roosevelt's first week in office they worked diligently, often for days without much sleep, and without fanfare. Their priority was to end the banking crisis and to ensure that the banks reopened without further hoarding. Wyatt would state some forty years later that, if he and others had advertised their role in the restoration of sound banking, "Roosevelt wouldn't go on with it," and that the holdovers did not wish to deprive Roosevelt of the credit for solving the banking crisis, especially not the tremendous success of the First Fireside Chat. "We were career men," reflected Wyatt, and added that "career man don't go out seeking publicity. They go on and do their job no matter which administration is in power, and they do it—it's just like the English civil service, we don't play any politics." However, Wyatt emphatically repeated that "it wasn't the Brain Trust that did that job" during the critical days of working on the proclamation to close the banks and formulating the emergency banking bill.[29]

Moley wrote the following in his diary on March 12, 1933:

> Will Woodin . . . cannot dispense with certain technical advice now available from the present personnel of the Treasury staff [Hoover's Treasury officials]. Awalt, the Comptroller of the Currency, for example, is an excellent man within his limits and there are many others like him. But it is clear that these men must be watched. Their bent of mind is to play with the big boys. And their advice must be used by someone with broad social vision and with a different philosophy from their own. They cannot be depended upon always to make right judgments, that is to say, they are in no sense willfully distorting things; but there is a natural bias to their advice and decisions.[30]

Still guarding the New Deal, Moley continued to fear at every juncture since November 1932 that Roosevelt would not withstand pressure from others and that the New Deal could be modified or even reversed. To illustrate his point, he used the case of the banks of the Brahmer Brothers in Minnesota. Although the conservative members of the Treasury considered these banks unsound, they did not consider them insolvent. Thus the question of their reopening was politically difficult. Moley claimed that entire banking chains in the West

> have been bled white by the Eastern banks and if, on Monday, and Tuesday, only the big banks in the East have opened, the new Administration will be accused of playing the old game. Conservatives argue that this is doing the sound thing. The liberals [say], that the thousands and thousands of depositors will suffer as a result of this policy. The Conservatives say this is too bad: but we have got to go through a process of terrible deflation in order to recover at all and that if we start making exceptions in favor of unsound banks, we will wreck the whole system. The liberals answer to hell with the

system, if it is going to be preserved solely in the interests of those who have been hurt least by what has happened.[31]

The ideological underpinnings are clearly visible here. In the midst of working out a plan to reopen the banks, Moley took a partisan view of the larger political terrain. He feared that the new administration would be seen, not for its courageous plan for reopening the banks and helping the many poor and unemployed, but for following the very plan outlined by the pro-banking Hoover administration. Moley worried about perceptions. After all, Roosevelt followed a conservative approach to solving the banking crisis, adding only a rhetorical dimension.

But Moley need not worry. Roosevelt's rhetorical plan was the decisive key to solving the banking crisis, though perhaps Moley could not appreciate it with all of Hoover's holdovers hovering around the president. Moley's snap judgment in the midst of the banking crisis would later be corrected as he praised the key Hoover holdovers, identifying each one of them—Ballantine, Wyatt, and Awalt—as the individuals who performed admirably in saving the banks. When preparing his book *The First New Deal,* Moley corresponded with Awalt in 1964, indicating to him that "my purpose is to show how, when Woodin and I appeared on the scene after Hoover and Roosevelt were completely deadlocked, we depended so completely upon the people in the Treasury, including Mills, Ballantine, and your good self. It would have been impossible for a new Administration, without leaning so heavily on the outgoing Administration, to have survived the crisis." And of the meeting in the Treasury on the night of March 3, 1933, Moley wrote some thirty years later that "everyone forgot political differences. Our concern was to save the banking system."[32]

In the final account, congressional passage of the Emergency Banking Act in a mere seven hours and a half was highly unusual and quite dramatic. As a result, Roosevelt could clearly show the nation significant progress, resilience, and determination, just as he had promised the nation two days earlier.

The First Fireside Chat

Following Roosevelt's decision on Thursday, March 9, to extend the bank holiday until the following Monday, Tuesday, or Wednesday, the secretary of the treasury issued a statement on March 10 to the effect that "immediate action has been taken by the President and the Secretary of the Treasury which will make possible the resumption of banking operation in substantial volume at a very early date."[1] This statement functioned as a confidence builder, indicating to the nation that the bank holiday was about to end. But such confidence-building measures were not enough to overcome the public psychology of fear. Roosevelt had one more item in his rhetorical bag.

Roosevelt's staff was told on Saturday, March 11, to prepare a draft for a radio address. On the same day, Roosevelt announced via the press that "the technical difficulties which operated to delay the opening of the banks have finally been substantially overcome," and that banks would reopen on March 13 in Federal Reserve cities, on March 14 in some 250 cities where clearing houses were operating, and on March 15 elsewhere.[2] In the same statement, Roosevelt prepared the nation for his radio address:

The Constitution has laid upon me the duty of conveying the condition of the country to the Congress assembled at Washington.

I believe I have a like duty to convey to the people themselves a clear picture of the situation at Washington itself whenever there is danger of any confusion as to what the Government is undertaking. That there may be a clear understanding as to just what has takevn place during the last two days since the passage of this Act it is my intention, over the national radio networks, at ten o'clock Sunday evening, to explain clearly and in simple language to all of you just what has been achieved and the sound reasons which underlie this declaration to you.[3]

This is a most accurate description of the radio address, in message, direction, style, and tone. The stated reason for delivering the speech was to explain and simplify the intricate and complicated banking system. It is significant that the stated reason for the speech was to inform the American people but not to persuade. The suasive objective would be the key to Roosevelt's national address, but he would achieve this objective subtly.

Roosevelt knew that, just as fear was a perceptual variable, so was the resumption of confidence, and that only through strong and effective leadership, displayed visually and substantively, would the nation trust its banking system again. For Roosevelt, effective leadership meant the projection of emphatic and active leadership attributes. Roosevelt presented himself as a caring president who understood the people's apprehension. He also knew that in times of great stress and apprehension the people needed a president who would present complex issues with simplicity and clarity, and thus he repeated several times that he would present a "simple" and "clear" message. Roosevelt also offered himself as the people's humble servant, who owed them an explanation. No longer would the people see an aloof and distant president, as was the case with Hoover. A week after inauguration, Roosevelt was seen as he planned all along: a markedly different president, direct, humble, and caring, at least compared to his predecessor. On his ethos were hanging all the banks and the people's belief that they and the banks were safe again.

Roosevelt's mastery of the art of timing foreshadowed his radio address. The very statement of confidence was meant to condition the

American people to accept the president's take on ending the banking crisis. In a similar vein, Secretary of the Treasury Woodin issued a statement on March 11 that authorized all federal land banks, federal intermediate credit banks, joint stock land banks, federal home loan banks, regional agricultural credit corporations, and the RFC to resume normal banking functions on Monday, March 13, at 9 o'clock A.M.[4] In short, banks would reopen at the start of the next week. Woodin also touched on the prospect of not opening all banks, declaring that "only sound institutions will be permitted to carry on all of their usual functions to the end that no bank shall be reopened for business on any basis that will run the risk of being forced to close again because of demands which it is not in a position to satisfy."[5]

The idea of Roosevelt speaking to the nation via a radio address had been discussed in general terms several months earlier. Merlin H. Aylesworth, president of the National Broadcasting Company, suggested as much to Roosevelt in a letter sent in December 1932. Aylesworth suggested a weekly radio address lasting about fifteen to twenty minutes.[6] This general plan was now urgently needed as Roosevelt sought a venue that would allow him to speak directly to the people, explaining the steps taken since Saturday and asking people to have confidence in their bank. The day and time, Sunday at 10:00 P.M., were considered optimal, given the different time zones, as not too late in the east and just after dinner time in the west.[7]

Who Drafted the First Fireside Chat?

Roosevelt often solicited input from several individuals for his upcoming speeches, asking advisers, assistants, speechwriters, and friends to forward drafts and thoughts about a given speech. In finalizing a speech, though, Roosevelt was the primary source of ideas, arguments, and the designated language. Yet the question of who drafted the First Fireside Chat presents no small mystery.[8] Charles Michelson, a staff member of the Democratic National Committee and frequent public relations troubleshooter, was the individual assigned to draft the radio address. It is not clear who suggested Michelson to Roosevelt, though Moley thinks that Stephen Early, Roosevelt's press secretary, may have been the one. Moley volunteered that "Roosevelt had never been happy with Michelson's compositions," but James MacGregor Burns writes that Michelson was "a superb publicity man" and a "ghost writer of scores of speeches that had slashed and pummeled the Hoover administration."[9]

Michelson had recently been called upon to help "explain" Rex Tugwell's ill-advised comments to one of Hoover's confidants in January 1933 about Roosevelt's knowledge of the severity of the banking crisis and his plan to do nothing until he assumed office. According to Michelson, he "was told to prepare an address for the President. This was the foundation of this fireside talk which electrified the country. I told Woodin and the others that I would need somebody to keep me straight on fiscal nomenclature, etc., exaggerating my own deficiency by telling them I did not know a debenture from a due bill. So they assigned a young man to sit up with me while I batted out on the typewriter the first draft of the document."[10] When he completed the draft, Michelson brought it to the White House.

According to Moley, he and Ballantine reviewed Michelson's draft and found it wanting.[11] Moley claims that he turned the task of re-working the draft to Ballantine, who in turn "substantially composed a new draft. Ballantine delivered this to Roosevelt. His recollection later was that he did not submit the Michelson alternative to Roosevelt," and that Roosevelt "then dictated a draft, with Ballantine's version before him."[12]

Moley's version of the drafting of the radio address prompted an exchange in the press between Ballantine and Michelson following Michelson's 1944 publication of *The Ghost Talks*. Michelson writes in this book that he first learned of Ballantine's involvement with the radio address from a book by Moley, and that he could only surmise that Moley was the one to give Ballantine the draft that he, Michelson, worked on. Michelson's account is that he went to the White House with his draft, that he did not see or hear from anyone else, and that Roosevelt lay on a couch and dictated his own speech.[13] Upon reading this account, Ballantine commenced correspondence with Walter Wyatt, checking accounts of events that took place some eleven years earlier and sharing an early draft of a response article he was planning to publish. Upon receiving the draft of the article, Wyatt replied to Ballantine in a lengthy letter, covering much more than just the drafting of the First Fireside Chat. In it, he reiterated that the "real job" during the banking crisis was done, not by "the swarm of college professors and 'braintrusters,'" but "in accordance with plans which had been crystallizing since February 12th" by the Hoover administration.[14]

Digressing from Ballantine's specific query, Wyatt added that "I shall give President Roosevelt full credit for the courage, political skill, and forensic ability with which he met the problem after his inauguration. . . . But the real hero of my story will be one of the 'holdovers' who forgot politics and personalities and took dear old Secretary Woodin by the hand, told him what to do, and served him and the country loyally, unselfishly and with great skill and success—one Arthur A. Ballantine." As for Michelson's account, Wyatt dismissed him altogether as an individual who simply "did not even know what was going on. . . . After a week or two, he came to me in desperation and begged me to keep him informed as to what was going on; but I gave him nothing."[15]

Ready with his notes cross-checked with some of Hoover's holdovers, Ballantine published an article in the *New York Herald Tribune* challenging Michelson's story. According to Ballantine, Michelson gave him the draft of the radio address on Saturday morning, and after reviewing it he concluded that it needed substantial revisions. Ballantine, observing that Michelson was quite fatigued, suggested that he go home and rest and that he, Ballantine, would rework the speech. Michelson, according to Ballantine, was happy to go home and rest. Ballantine stated that he revised the draft and took it to Roosevelt. Ballantine did not recall taking Michelson's draft to the president, though he did not know how Roosevelt finalized the speech since he was not present when the final draft was composed. Ballantine did, however, suggest that his draft was "extensively used in giving form to his telling presentation."[16]

But Ballantine may have been aided in drafting the First Fireside Chat. In a letter to Ballantine on August 1, 1944, Wyatt wrote that

"Goldenweiser says Bud Stark wrote the first draft." And in "Notes on Conversation, August 1, 1944 with Goldenweiser re Bank Holiday," Ballantine wrote an identical account: "As to the President's Speech, Goldenweiser said the first draft was written by Bud Stark; but that it obviously was rewritten before it was delivered. Goldenweiser does not now claim credit for any part of the President's Speech and says he never saw it until after it was delivered."[17]

It appears, then, that initial drafting of the First Fireside Chat was done by one Bud Stark, who worked in the office of Goldenweiser, researcher of the Federal Reserve Board. It is not clear if Ballantine requested the initial draft. This account itself seems detached from Ballantine's version, and it surfaced only when Wyatt suggested that Ballantine look further into the matter. One can surmise that perhaps a general call for help in drafting the speech went out to several Treasury officials and that Ballantine, entrusted with drafting the speech, finalized his version after the initial work of others. The possibility that several Treasury individuals influenced the drafting of the First Fireside Chat gains credence when one recalls that Awalt's phrasing also found its way into the speech.

Moley would write several years later that Roosevelt's first presidential radio address clearly showed how fully he was briefed by Ballantine and Woodin. Journalist John Flynn, who wrote a critical account of the Roosevelt myth, thought he put the question of who drafted the First Fireside Chat to rest: "One feature about the address remains unknown to most people to this day and that is that it was written, not by Roosevelt or any member of his Brain Trust, but by Arthur Ballantine, Under-Secretary of the Treasury under Hoover, who with Ogden Mills, his chief, had remained at the Treasury to help pilot the country through its famous banking crisis."[18] Biographer Freidel reaches a similar assessment, stating that, though Michelson wrote the first draft, Roosevelt discarded this draft and followed the draft written by Ballantine.[19] I do not reject this account, but I believe that other Treasury officials, including Stark, Goldenweiser, and Awalt, helped with the initial drafting of the speech and that Ballantine finalized the draft and then forwarded it to Roosevelt, independent of Michelson's work on the speech. It is unfortunate that Ballantine's draft of the First Fireside Chat has apparently disappeared. In commenting on the drafting of the speech in 1944, neither Ballantine nor Moley made any reference to the actual text of the speech draft, thus depriving scholars of the opportunity to study the relationship between that draft and Roosevelt's final version.

Neither Michelson, Ballantine, Freidel, nor any other historian or biographer has accounted for how Roosevelt finalized the First Fireside Chat. One individual, however, Francis Gloyd Awalt, shed some light on the preparation of the address. Awalt revealed for the first time in 1969 that on Saturday, March 11, he was asked by Woodin to accompany him to the White House for a meeting with Roosevelt. When he arrived he found Adolph Miller, governor of the Federal Reserve Board, and Louis M. Howe, Roosevelt's trusted aide. Roosevelt asked the three "to be seated around his desk and explained that he wanted to read to us the speech he intended to deliver to the nation on the following evening, Sunday, March 12." Awalt recalled being seated to Roosevelt's right, Woodin to the president's left, and Miller across. Louis M. Howe stood by the window.[20]

Roosevelt read the entire speech and then turned to his Treasury officials for their opinions. Woodin considered the speech "great," and Miller thought it was "excellent." Awalt's account is most revealing. Not knowing the "President's disposition too well," Awalt writes, he "rushed in, as a fool where angels fear to tread, and said that it was a fine speech but—. This was as far as I got when the President snapped 'But what?' I told him that he had stated we would open only sound banks and, in our hurry to complete the program, there might be some exceptions. He stated in no uncertain terms that that was what we were going to do, 'open only sound banks.' I had nothing more to say."[21] Though it is not clear just how much editing Roosevelt did, we do know that three Treasury officials heard a complete draft of the radio talk a day earlier.

The finalization of the First Fireside Chat was also influenced by several telegrams from state governors, all cabled on March 12, only hours prior to the broadcast. The governors were particularly concerned with the solvency of state banks and their plight relative to federal banks. Ben Ross, governor of Idaho, cabled Roosevelt on March 12 at 7:15 P.M. to state that it was "imperative if our section of country is to be saved that state banks which are non members of federal reserve system be given same consideration as members and national banks." Albert C. Ritchie, governor of Maryland, cabled Roosevelt at 7:06 P.M.: "I earnestly and respectfully appeal to you to declare for equality of treatment for the state banks in your broadcast tonight." Henry Horner, governor of Illinois, cabled at 7:53 P.M., suggesting to Roosevelt "that it is important to the state banking problems of this state and other states that you declare for equality of treatment of state banks with national banks. If you could do so in your radio broadcast tonight it would help mightily and be agreeably received." Gifford Pinchot, governor of Pennsylvania, cabled at 8:39 P.M. that "the unfortunate impression is spreading here that federal authorities may overlook the interest of state banks. Since eighty three percent of Pennsylvania banks with forty eight percent of all deposits are non members of federal reserve system this is important. Reassuring from you tonight over radio would be most valuable." And Hill Macalister, governor of Tennessee, cabled at 7:56 P.M. to urge Roosevelt to ensure that "the federal banking policy shall provide equality of treatment of state banks with those organized under federal law."[22]

State governors were concerned enough that they appear to have followed a similar line of argument, urging the president to include a statement in his radio talk about state banks grounded on the principle of "equality of treatment." Their fear was that the president would focus only on federal banks, leaving governors responsible for their respective state banks and likely unable to provide the necessary funds to reopen them. The governors' cables also illustrate that fear and uncertainties, just hours prior to reopening the banks, was significantly high. Roosevelt would take the governors' concern seriously and include the necessary statement to allay them.

Roosevelt's own account of the drafting of his First Fireside Chat is vague yet instructive. To a query by Helen Wilkinson Reynolds, editor of the Dutchess County Historical Society, who in 1933 asked the president "to clarify the origin of the speech," Roosevelt replied that he "asked three or four gentlemen connected with the government to let me have in writing their thoughts on what I should say in a public radio statement." After getting informal input from friends, he sat by his desk and "tried to picture a mason at work on a new building, a girl behind a counter, and a farmer in his field. . . . The net result was the dictation of a radio talk to these people."[23]

Roosevelt did not identify the individuals who helped draft the radio address. As with his first inaugural address, he sought to convey the impression that he was the author of this radio talk as well. But the account of this talk is consistent with approaches to the drafting of other speeches: he solicited drafts and ideas from several individuals and used the various suggestions to write the final speech. This account is also instructive for our understanding of how Roosevelt constructed his audience. Roosevelt imagined three individuals, all working-class people taken from construction, service, and farming. Notwithstanding the fact that his imagined audience was made out of the millions who elected him, Roosevelt's constructed audience comprised hardworking individuals struggling to earn enough to sustain their households, those whose hard-earned money deposited in the banks was of utmost concern.

The selection of these three imagined individuals indicates that Roosevelt understood the plight of millions, their fear and their need for a quick restoration of confidence in the government and its leader. His address would thus focus on understanding the causes of fear and, consistent with the message of the inaugural address, he would also point to the gap between fear and reality. Roosevelt would also explain the causes of the banking crisis and anchor the resumed solvency on the new administration's ability to come up with a workable plan that would help the nation in a matter of days. Roosevelt understood that time was of the essence and that the people were now asking for a quick solution. His address would thus revolve around time as a master metaphor and the subtext of the radio address.

Addressing the Nation

Only a week into office, Roosevelt's credibility was on the line, and he had to ensure that his plan was believable. He also had to appear markedly different from his predecessor. Above all else, the speech required more than an attitude change. It required immediate action. Thus Roosevelt opted for a transparent address that described the chronology of events that led to the banking crisis and outlined the specific plan for restoring confidence in the banks. He also opted for a pedagogical speech, the kind taken by a teacher who imparts an important lesson. The speech's style was distinctly personal and affable but also direct. Roosevelt correctly assessed his audience as eager to hear about specific measures that would allow them to assess the banks' solvency in order to decide whether to withdraw or deposit money. Absent proof of the banks' solvency, the proof available was in the credibility of the president's plan. Here Roosevelt would show his rhetorical mastery, speaking over the radio, more like a teacher who embarks on a profound lesson than a president whose language assumes the high office he occupies.

When Roosevelt was ready to read his speech over the radio, no one could find the reading copy of the speech. The reading copy was never found and to this day it is missing from Roosevelt's papers in the presidential library. Roosevelt's secretary, Grace Tully, confirmed that the First Fireside Chat "is one of the few addresses of which there is no official record since the reading original never was found."[24]

"The President's March," by John Philip Sousa, opened the radio program and an announcer introduced the president: "Ladies and Gentlemen: The President of the United States."[25] Roosevelt took a mimeographed copy of the speech from one of the newspaperman seated in the White House basement, "mashed out a cigarette stub, turned to the microphone, and began."[26]

The very beginning of the radio address signaled the unique relationship the president sought to foster. He did not begin his address with a salutary recognition of the audience, time, or place, and an appropriate "Good evening" was not to be heard. Instead Roosevelt opted for establishing the rhetorical immediacy between speaker and listener. "I want to talk for a few moments," started the president, to commence a frank talk between neighbors. This immediacy was essential for perceiving Roosevelt as a different kind of president, empathetic, down to earth, and understanding. The corresponding intimate style was the key in creating closeness between the president and the people.

The need for the frank talk was quickly rationalized as informational in essence: There are "few who understand the mechanics of banking" relative to the "overwhelming majority who use banks for the making of deposits and the drawing of checks" (1).[27] The informative objective of the address was elaborated further: "I want to tell you what has been done in the last few days, why it was done, and what the next steps are going to be" (1). Roosevelt also told his radio listeners that the many statements by state officials, legislatures, and those appearing in Treasury regulations, "couched for the most part in banking and legal terms," should now "be explained for the benefit of the average citizen" (1).

Simplicity and directness were the hallmarks of this speech; it would not be just like others heard many times before. This would be a different speech—simple, direct, and informative. Above all else, this would be a persuasive speech and a powerful one, but the persuasion would be subtle. Roosevelt quickly related to the American people, telling them that he had only them in mind, and to make this point most emphatic he added: "I owe this in particular because of the fortitude and good temper with which everybody has accepted the inconvenience and hardships of the banking holiday" (1). This gratitude and forthcoming sentiments were most unprecedented. The president acknowledged the hardships many had to endure during the banking crisis, and the least he could do during these dire times was to explain to them in simple terms the causes of the banking crisis and the remedies planned. What was not stated but was very much the subtext was that this simple explanation could be the difference between further panic and the eventual collapse of the nation's financial institutions and the restoration of stability and confidence in the banking system and the U.S. economy.

Roosevelt was a crafty rhetorician. Not only did he inform the American people what he was going to tell them and the reasons for telling them, he also told them that he knew that they understood "what we in Washington have been about." This directness, which characterizes many of Roosevelt's speeches, allowed him to construct an intimate contact with his audience. Indeed, the many letter writers would point exactly to his directness and intimacy as among the primary reasons for appreciating the speech. Their letters (considered in detail in chapter 7) cover all rhetorical variables including message, delivery, style, tone, appeals, and character. The letter writers are personal, touching, and revealing of the nation's fears and aspirations. Many commented on the effectiveness of the speech, its simple language, direct style, heart-to-heart and intimate appeal. Some found God's hand in this inspirational address, while others highlighted how quickly Roosevelt restored confidence in the nation. Many also praised the president as a skilled radio announcer, suggesting that he use radio occasionally to address them on important issues.

Roosevelt purposefully used the first person "I" and addressed the American people as "you" to project intimacy and a conversational style. He visualized his radio audience "as being few people around his fireside, and the public imagines [him] setting comfortably at his desk, conversing easily in their living rooms."[28]

Rhetoric scholars would likewise confirm that Roosevelt had a knack for developing addresses that had a "direct quality which characterized all his speaking," and that "he was able to establish intimate contact with his audience."[29] The tribute and recognition of the people's virtues were sure to empower them. With such tribute Roosevelt could ask the people to "continue to have your cooperation as fully as I have had your sympathy and help during the past week" (1). Roosevelt did not wish to appear to take for granted the people's cooperation he so badly needed. He could only hope that the sympathy and receptiveness shown during Inauguration Day could now be extended into active cooperation. False humility or innate confidence, Roosevelt had to walk a delicate line that made it clear to the American people that their trust and behavior would determine the course of the banking crisis and that he, the president, needed first to apprise them of the situation. Persuasion could not be more crucial yet so simple and direct.

The banking situation had to be explained in rudimentary terms, first by describing the essence of banking: "When you deposit money in the bank the bank does not put the money into a safe deposit vault" (1). This simple truism probably escaped many who could not understand why money deposited could not be withdrawn. The money deposited, Roosevelt explained, is invested in bonds, commercial paper, mortgages, and other loans. The deposited money, then, is used by the banks to move the "wheels of industry and agriculture," and only a small portion of it remains in the bank in the form of currency and in amount adequate and necessary for "normal times" (1). With this simple explanation Roosevelt sought to have people understand that money deposited does not stay as such and that only a small fraction of the money deposited stays in the form of currency for normal withdrawal purposes.

But these were not "normal times." Roosevelt described the events of the past few weeks as an unusual development born of the "undermined confidence on the part of the public," and hence "a general rush by a large portion of our population to turn bank deposits into currency or gold—a rush so great that the soundest banks could not get enough currency to meet the demand" (1). Neither could the banks, added the president, "sell perfectly sound assets of a bank and convert them into cash except at panic prices far below their real value" (2). This simple description of essential banking practices must have been an eye opener to many. Roosevelt sought to minimize the extent and severity of the crisis by arguing that many banks failed not because they lacked the necessary liquidity but simply because they could not sell sound assets on short notice. Bank failures, then, were much less complex than they appeared, and if people understood several relatively simple facts, they would see the relative simplicity of the crisis and be willing to accept the plan Roosevelt put forward. The crisis scene, created by the failure of only a few banks, brought unnecessary panic and pressure on sound banks. But Roosevelt added an interesting twist. He presented a tension between private needs for currency and the nation's interest in solid banking, hoping that responsible citizenry would side with the larger needs of the nation.

Now, Roosevelt hoped that many could understand why running to their banks to withdraw money would be futile and harmful to the larger interest of the nation's industry and agriculture. The banks and bankers had been caught in the psychology of panic, and limited in their ability to keep the panic in check. Implied in the description was the moral of the story: there is no place for private and selfish interests compared with the nation's economic needs. The situation had so deteriorated, described Roosevelt, that by March 3 "scarcely a bank in the country was open to do business," and to face this deteriorating situation state governors issued "proclamations temporarily closing them [the banks] in whole or in part" (2).[30] The date March 3 is important; it was Hoover's last full day in office. Roosevelt was fully aware that the blame for the banking crisis would fall on the shoulders of his predecessor, giving some credence to Hoover's accusation that Roosevelt was purposefully letting the crisis intensify and climax so that he could offer a solution at the most critical point, when resistance would be very limited if not muted altogether.

Roosevelt described the sequence of events leading to the banking collapse, making it clear that only after the state governors closed banks in their respective states did he issue a proclamation "providing for the nation-wide bank holiday, and this was the first step in the Government's reconstruction of our financial and economic fabric" (2). Indeed, state governors were reached by Treasury officials on the night of March 3 and in the wee hours of Inauguration Day, March 4, when Hoover was still the president. Roosevelt would take count of every hour to ensure that, with the series of actions taken, he would be seen as the savior of the nation's banking collapse.

The second step in solving the banking crisis, Roosevelt told the nation, was Congress confirming the proclamation closing the banks and, most important, "broadening my powers so that it became possible in view of the requirement of time to extend the holiday and lift the ban of that holiday gradually" (2). The crisis required quick action, and action now meant decisive leadership. Roosevelt's straightforward description of broadening his power (without detailing or even mentioning the Trading with the Enemy Act of 1917) was meant to convince the American people that they finally had a president able and willing to make the tough call. And the tough call he made, telling the people that both Republicans and Democrats "showed . . . a devotion to public welfare and a realization of the emergency and the necessity for speed that it is difficult to match in our history" (2). Roosevelt was correct: No such emergency power had been granted to a president except during wartime; no president had asked for such a provision except in war, and this very extension of a war statute to an economic crisis was a stretch that explains, at least in part, Hoover's hesitancy.

Roosevelt had shown no such hesitancy. The banking crisis was as threatening as a war, if not worse. And if the extension of the 1917 act to an economic crisis was a stretch, Roosevelt took care of that by couching his rhetoric in war metaphors.[31] With the special provision broadening his power, Roosevelt was able to do with much speed that which his predecessor failed—to bring unity to Congress, a body known for lengthy and tedious deliberations, to pass a major piece of legislation in a matter of hours.

Whereas Hoover's rhetoric and action exemplified the extent to which he let the scene control the situation, Roosevelt controlled the scene. The implication was clear—Roosevelt's action displayed unmatched courage and ability. And in controlling and even dictating the scene, Roosevelt incorporated the central metaphor of his presidency—"public welfare." Despite the continuous pressure from Hoover and the fear that the banking crisis might modify or cancel the New Deal, Roosevelt sent a clear statement that his central program was intact and that the crisis scene would not modify the principles of the New Deal that propelled him to the presidency. The "public welfare" metaphor meant espousing an economy that would benefit more individuals, a hint that inflationary measures would increase prices and in turn restart industrial productivity. Also implied in this plan was that inflationary measures would mean getting off the gold standard.

The third step Roosevelt outlined for solving the banking crisis was the series of regulations that permitted banks to continue some essential functions such as the distribution of food, allowing for the purchases of household necessities, and permitting the payment of payrolls. In other words, the decisive actions were, not arbitrary and cold, but humane and considerate of the many difficulties people suffered as a result of bank closures. Indeed, Roosevelt acknowledged the many difficulties and inconveniences resulting from the bank holiday, but closing the banks afforded the government "the opportunity to supply the currency necessary to meet the situation" (2). The crux of the banking situation, taken from Awalt's draft of the message to Congress, was put most succinctly: "No sound bank is a dollar worse off than it was when it closed its doors last Monday. Neither is any bank which may turn out not to be in a position for immediate opening" (2). If the restoration of confidence was the essential message, Roosevelt gave the people the very dose they needed. The classification of banks to be reopened, both sound and not-so-sound banks, covered the majority of the banks.

To add further evidence that many banks were or would be solvent and ready to reopen, Roosevelt stated that the twelve Federal Reserve Banks would "issue additional currency on good assets and thus the banks which reopen will be able to meet every legitimate call," and that the Bureau of Engraving and Printing (a name Roosevelt corrected in the text) would supply new currency in large volume "to every part of the country." Finally, and with great assurance, Roosevelt declared that the currency coming from the Federal Reserve "is sound currency because it is backed by actual, good assets" (3).

This radio address can be read as one extended argument supported by subarguments and calculated to lay to rest all potential counterarguments. The primary argument advanced is that most banks were solvent and would reopen, that many banks that were not fully solvent would become solvent and reopen as well, that the government would supply additional currency to ensure that banks that could be reopened would be able to handle all depositors' demands, and that the supply of additional currency was backed by good assets.

Anticipating a concern over why all the banks that could be reopened would not be reopened at the same time, Roosevelt stated that banks would open gradually in order not to repeat "another epidemic of bank failures" (3). Ever keen on using medical metaphors, Roosevelt's answer was not altogether convincing. One can assume that the missing logical leap lies in the psychological variable inherent to economic behavior—that fear and panic appear in the face of uncertainty. Thus, a gradual reopening of banks allows for confidence building and a safety measure against potential panic. Once depositors realized that their money was safe or that they could withdraw any amount they needed, the word would quickly spread and calm jittery depositors elsewhere.

The gradual plan called for reopening on Monday, March 13, banks in good shape located in the twelve Federal Reserve Bank cities; reopening the following day about 250 sound banks in cities where clearing houses were located (allowing for a quick assessment of assets); and reopening Wednesday and thereafter of many smaller banks subject to the government's survey of their solvency. Extending the time to reopen many small banks, Roosevelt explained, was necessary in order to give such banks time to apply for additional loans, to obtain the necessary currency, and for the government to verify these banks' ability to handle all depositors' demands. In short, common sense dictated an orderly reopening of banks.

To allay any concern that banks that would not reopen on Monday would reopen on Tuesday or Wednesday, Roosevelt told his listeners that they were "by no means justified in believing that it will not open," and that "a bank that opens on one of the subsequent days is in exactly the same status as the bank that opens tomorrow" (4). The psychological foundation of economic behavior was central to Roosevelt's plan to restore faith and confidence in basic banking practices. The gradual reopening of banks based on levels of solvency and liquidity, from the soundest to those in need of reorganization, was the key to regaining lost confidence. And though the initial classification of banks into A, B, and C clearly guided this address, Roosevelt avoided mentioning this strict classification.

Most of the people's worries centered on banks that did not belong to the Federal Reserve System. Roosevelt assured the American people, just as several state governors had suggested, that these banks "will receive assistance from member banks and from the Reconstruction Finance Corporation" (4). The only difference between member banks and those not belonging to the Federal Reserve System was that the licenses to resume operation of the latter would be granted by state authorities. Yet, to maintain a consistent system of opening banks, the states were asked by the secretary of the treasury to allow for the reopening of good banks on the same schedule as the national banks. Note that Roosevelt qualified the reopening of only "good" banks, implying but never stating the worse classification of some banks.

To those "who have not recovered from their fear" and who "may again begin withdrawals" from their accounts once banks were open, Roosevelt sent a clear message: "The banks will take care of all needs except, of course, the hysterical demands of hoarders—and it is my belief that hoarding during the past week has become an exceedingly unfashionable pastime" (4). That in a week's time Roosevelt could talk about an "unfashionable pastime" showed his confidence in his rhetorical ability to change public sentiments quickly. Labeling hoarders "hysterical" was a safe suggestive device that pit reasonable individuals against hoarders who acted out of panic. Persuasion was in high demand, and Roosevelt could not afford to err in this crucial address. "It needs no prophet to tell you that when the people find that they can get their money—that they can get it when they want it for all legitimate purposes—the phantom of fear will soon be laid" (4). The "It" was the situation, namely, the fear that the money in the banks was not safe and that banks' failure would continue. Fear could be erased by convincing people of its unreasonable, even hysterical nature, whereas the opposite sentiments exemplified confidence.

Roosevelt first described fear metaphorically, as a curable disease that some were yet to "recover" from. In the following sentence fear took on a battle metaphor, depicted as a "phantom" soon "to be laid." Roosevelt was the physician who would heal the nation from the disease of fear. He was also the fearless leader who would slay fear forever. Health, vigor, and fearlessness were the attributes Roosevelt assigned to himself in the midst of the banking crisis. He had used the metaphorical cluster of health and vigor for the past eight years, primarily to overcome the perception that his physical disability would impede political potential.[32] Now Roosevelt found the utility of this cluster in dealing with a fearful nation. The shift in metaphorical quality signaled Roosevelt's concern for the very essence of the banking crisis—fear. The metaphorical shift also afforded Roosevelt the opportunity to counter fear twice: once by describing it as curable, thus transcending the basic economic malady; and then by describing it as a "phantom," therefore unreal and unjustified, just as he did in the inaugural address. The people could select the metaphor that appealed to their senses.

To overcome any continued fear, Roosevelt told the American people that banks were safe and that everyone would be able to withdraw the money they needed. Most crucial, Roosevelt told the people that the banks were safe even before their reopening. This level of confidence was essential despite the fact that no one could guarantee how people would behave once the banks opened. As with deliberative speaking, the future could not be dictated but only projected, hence its generic limitation. Given this very limitation, confidence in the banking system had to rest on the confidence the audience had in the speaker and in his plan of action. In short, Roosevelt asked the people to have faith in him. This is precisely what Roosevelt sought to achieve. He prophesied that the banks were safe and that all depositors' demands would be satisfied. He could not say more than that. Evidence that the banks would not experience another failure was transcended by confidence and faith in the president, who hoped that actions he took since assuming office would persuade the public that he knew what he was doing.

The key to a successful reopening of the banks lay not only in preventing additional hoarding but, more important, in ensuring that many would leave their deposits for the long haul and consider bank accounts the safest mode of saving. To that end, Roosevelt reiterated his belief that many "will again be glad to have their money where it will be safely taken care of and where they can use it conveniently at any time. I can assure you that it is safer to keep your money in a reopened bank than under a mattress" (4–5). So simple a request was foundational to the entire economic system, and Roosevelt minced no words expressing the gravity of his request: "The success of our whole great national program depends, of course, upon the cooperation of the public—on its intelligent support and use of a reliable system" (5).

The future of the U.S. economy depended on public support, not mere support, but intelligent support brought upon by a reliable system just put into action by the new administration.

Two rhetorical devices operated here: a causal relationship whereby a reliable system, a euphemism for the administration's plan to reopen the banks, would be seen as practical, sound, and fair, thus inducing people to see the wisdom of trusting that which is reliable; and the use of an enthymeme ("presenting an argument in such a way that the audience participates in its completion")[33] whereby the people are told that they are intelligent, and since an intelligent being would leave the money in the banks, people should leave their money in the banks. With the attribute of intelligence, Roosevelt empowered people to do what he requested of them.

Seeking to convince people of the solvency of the banks was a matter of faith in the president, in his presentation, in his character, and in the actions he had taken over the past week. Economic measures were designed to guarantee a successful reopening of banks—making it possible "for banks more readily to convert their assets into cash than was the case before," introducing "more liberal provision . . . for issuing currency on the security of these good assets," convincing people that "this currency is not fiat currency," and that it had been issued against "adequate security—and every good bank has an abundance of such security" (5). And though the future was only some twelve hours away, no evidence was possible that the banks' reopening would be stable and hoarding would cease, as Roosevelt predicted. Roosevelt had no other rhetorical venue but to repeat the strategy he had already used: the actions taken by the government would ensure the banks' solvency, and people would have faith in these measures.

"One more point before I close," Roosevelt cautioned: "There will be, of course, some banks unable to reopen without being reorganized. The new law allows the Government to assist in making these reorganizations quickly and effectively and even allows the Government to subscribe to at least a part of a new capital which may be required" (5). Roosevelt must have known that many had in mind this banking category as the most worrisome, so he opted for lessening the importance of this banking category. He also sought to minimize concern over banks in difficulties with assurances that the new legislation Congress just passed permitted the infusion of new capital, making it clear that Roosevelt would not allow them to falter. Just as he told Awalt the previous day, the banking categories the president outlined did not include banks that could not be opened; all banks that were to reopen were considered solvent.

Indeed, Roosevelt's objective was to project confidence based on the people's observation "of what your government is doing," adding that "there is nothing complex, or radical in the process." Simplicity and practicality were to be the hallmarks of the new administration, with a clear emphasis on quick actions. The week that commenced with the inaugural address and concluded with the First Fireside Chat was to be taken as an unfolding rhetorical text designed to project an active, decisive, and confident administration doing everything possible to recover from the banking crisis. The "elemental recital" of the steps undertaken to reopen the banks was nothing short of convincing people that the serious crisis was now manageable, that the banks would reopen, that the government was functioning again, and that at its helm stood a strong leader who would ensure that all would be well again and soon.

Still, Roosevelt was not done persuading the people that the banks were sound. After enumerating the various processes the government had taken to ensure the reopening of as many banks as possible, he returned to the theme of his inaugural address. He acknowledged, albeit with strategic word choice, that "we had a bad banking situation." Now the banking failure was not a crisis but a situation, and the situation was not catastrophic but only bad. The use of "bad" afforded the identification of the guilty party. Indeed, the culprits were "incompetent and dishonest" bankers who "used the money entrusted to them in speculations and unwise loans" (6). These maladies were not true of the majority of the bankers, said Roosevelt, but "it was true in enough of them to shock the people for a time into a sense of insecurity." The "acts of comparatively few had tainted them all" (6). Assigning motives to a specific group was rhetorically advantageous; it positioned the president as the champion of the people's interests. Roosevelt sought to persuade the people that the banking situation could have been a limited one had it not been for the psychological effect that exacerbated the situation.

Unlike the depiction of bankers in the inaugural address as unscrupulous "money changers," here the culprit net was not cast so widely. Instead, Roosevelt emphasized that only few bankers tainted the entire banking industry. Roosevelt needed the bankers if he wanted to reopen the banks on solid financial footing. He also needed the bankers' cooperation given his conservative approach to solving the crisis at hand by securing liquidity and assets to guarantee depositors' funds. He did not plan to reform the banking system, at least not in his first week in office.

This is not an indictment of Roosevelt's policies. The banking crisis required a quick solution, whereas a complete reformation would have taken longer and lengthened the crisis unnecessarily. In any case, Roosevelt could not plan an overall banking reform in a matter of days. With these constraints, solving the banking crisis necessitated a highly effective rhetoric that could transcend the immediate and limited measures undertaken. Roosevelt acknowledged as much, stating that "it was the Government's job to straighten out this situation and do it as quickly as possible" (6). The banking "situation," nuanced Roosevelt again, was an abnormality that his administration came in to "straighten out." Again Roosevelt downplayed the severity of a crisis that only a few weeks earlier he described in a letter to Hoover as a fire that would spread no matter what the government did. Now he was in charge, and time was crucial. Hoover, probably listening on the radio like many Americans, must have cringed at hearing this account.

Roosevelt left the most troubling bank category—those that could not reopen—last on his list, stating that "I do not promise you that every bank will be reopened or that individual losses will not be suffered" (5). Presenting this group as an afterthought, he phrased such an eventuality, the most feared of all, to minimize its dire consequences. People could glean from this statement that perhaps a few banks would not reopen. But after the long list of all other banking classifications at different levels of solvency, the people were bound to regard the most severe cases as of negligible consequence. Roosevelt was quick, though, to assure his listeners that "there will be no losses that possibly could be avoided; and there would have been more and greater losses had we continued do drift" (6).

Thus, Roosevelt presented a benevolent leadership that had done all it could to minimize losses, though some losses could not be avoided. He sought to assure the people of the minority of losses to be incurred relative to those already avoided through quick action by the government. To alleviate any lingering concern over insolvent banks, Roosevelt went religious, telling his audience that he could "even promise you salvation for some at least of the sorely pressed banks. We shall be engaged not merely in reopening sound banks but in the creation of sound banks through reorganization" (6). Roosevelt announced that even banks in great difficulties would reopen once they had been reorganized. His retort to Awalt a day earlier about opening only solvent banks was very much the central theme of the First Fireside Chat.

The radio address ended the way it began, with Roosevelt humbly telling his many listeners how "wonderful" it was "to catch the note of confidence from all over the country. I can never be sufficiently grateful to the people for the loyal support they have given me in their acceptance of the judgment that has dictated our course, even though all our processes may not have seemed clear to them" (7). Of course, the American people were yet to show their confidence in the form of resuming normal banking behavior, leaving their money in the banks and perhaps even returning currency and gold withdrawn earlier. But to be on the safe side, Roosevelt assumed as much, knowing very well that presaging confidence was in itself an act of confidence. Put differently, if Roosevelt had confidence in the people, the people surely would reciprocate.

Confidence was the operative word for the duration of the banking crisis, and confidence was the rhetorical currency necessary for resuming a normal and stable banking industry. Roosevelt's straightforward address spelled out this very dictum:

After all there is an element in the re-adjustment of our financial system more important than currency, more important than gold, and that is the confidence of the people. Confidence and courage are the essentials of success in carrying out our plan. You people must have faith; you must not be stampeded by rumors or guesses. Let us unite in banishing fear. We have provided the machinery to restore our financial system; it is up to you to support and make it work. It is your problem no less than it is mine. Together we cannot fail. (7)

Like a teacher seeking to impart a tough but necessary lesson, Roosevelt put the onus of what would happen on Monday morning on the people. He had done his best, and the rest was in their hands. He repeated the call of his inaugural address to banish fear and assume faith. He also told them that economics was much more than a technical system based on cold mathematical formulas; it was a human system heavily dependent on human perceptions and confidence in a system's integrity.

The radio address, situated in one of the most serious challenges to America's survival, was direct and simple. It was devoid of technical jargon, superfluous statements, or novel eloquence. There was no need for embellishment or grand oratory. The people understood the serious situation, and all were hoping for practical solutions. Roosevelt understood the rhetorical situation and gave the people an address that could restore confidence by virtue of decisive and quick actions. Such a speech required a heavy dose of logical appeal, the kind that could sustain a common sense rhetoric.

The timing of the First Fireside Chat is crucial. Although Roosevelt had a pressing week, he could have given the address at another time or even a day earlier. That he opted for Sunday night, less than twelve hours before the banks reopened, is significant. Roosevelt was always known for his mastery of timing, and one has to assume that this factor did not escape him on this important issue. By addressing the American people the night before the start of the week, Roosevelt likely calculated that the dramatic address would yield the dramatic results he hoped for. He may have considered a late-night address heard by many weary and tired people as suasively advantageous, thinking that when people woke up the following morning the confidence generated by the address the night before would be translated to confidence in the banking system. Finally, Roosevelt may have considered a Sunday address advantageous for its religious significance, perhaps assuming that many anxious to hear of his plan would consider a Sunday address divinely inspired.

David M. Ryfe contends that Roosevelt "displayed a remarkable capacity to shift roles in the chats," and that in the First Fireside Chat he took the dual role of a person offering information and an expert instructing the American people on what was the best course of action. He also suggests that Roosevelt's use of pronouns was rhetorically advantageous because it allowed him to develop a specific sense of agency as well as identity.[34] In assuming these roles, primarily through the use of the pronoun "I," Roosevelt positioned himself as an observer who was credible enough to offer advice, an observer with enough rhetorical distance from the presidential role that he did not engage in too forceful a persuasion. Perhaps intuitively, Roosevelt knew that, given the intense and even emotional crisis associated with the fear of losing one's earnings, a forceful persuasion could backfire and a suggestive and instructive presentation had a better chance of success.

Studying Roosevelt's speech rate, Halford R. Ryan concludes that his First Fireside Chat was the slowest of all his radio addresses, and that Roosevelt's radio addresses in general were slower than his average speaking rate. One explanation for the slower rate of speaking over the radio is that Roosevelt intended to "elongate, to prolong his vowels and consonants," and that by doing so he was able "to communicate trust, competency, and tranquility."[35]

Roosevelt's strategy of empowering people to make the right decision about the soundness of the banks was possible by the frequent references to "you." This pronoun functioned to allow people to see themselves in control of the decision to withdraw or to keep their money in the banks. This very identity of responsible citizens became the agency through which Roosevelt would solve the banking crisis—the identity of confident Americans.

———————— ◆•◆•◆ ————————

The Citizens' Letters

In a cartoon from March 10, 1933, by H. M. Talburt in the *New York World-Telegram*, Roosevelt is portrayed as a lion trainer, standing on his two feet inside the cage with the lion roaring at him. The caption, a take on March's fickle weather, reads, "And you're going out like a lamb."[1] Notwithstanding Roosevelt's disability and wheelchair, he would tame the lion—the banking crisis—and the month that began under most ominous conditions would end mildly with the crisis quickly dissipating. Such confidence in Roosevelt's ability to solve the banking crisis two days before the First Fireside Chat portended its success. The growing confidence that the crisis would end soon was equally matched by accolades for accomplishing a difficult task.

Indeed, assessments of Roosevelt's First Fireside Chat are overwhelmingly positive but revealing nonetheless. One scholar writes that the radio address "was a masterpiece of clear, simple, effective exposition. Like the Inaugural Address, it produced an electric effect upon the people."[2] Biographer Freidel writes that the speech was "a simple talk, unadorned with the flights of rhetoric, or patriotic generalities that usually characterized presidential addresses. Undoubtedly its effectiveness lay in its simplicity and in Roosevelt's calm, earnest delivery." And, concludes Freidel, "it was most striking in contrast with the remote formalism of Roosevelt's predecessors, Hoover and Coolidge."[3] The fireside chats would be described by historian Burns as "Roosevelt's most important link with the people," their effectiveness explained by his ability to assume "the role of a father talking with his great family."[4] Historian David Kennedy, providing a more historical view, opines that "the results of Roosevelt's magic with the Congress and the people were immediately apparent," and that the "prolonged banking crisis, acute since at least 1930, with roots reaching back through the 1920s and even into the days of Andrew Jackson, was at last over."[5] For adviser Moley, capitalism "was saved in eight days."[6]

The individuals who worked in close proximity to Roosevelt during his first week in office were quite complimentary of the First Fireside Chat. Wyatt would comment some years later that it was

one of the most dramatic things that I ever saw. Before the bank holiday, the states declared a Bank Holiday . . . before all the Federal Reserve Banks closed March 4th. There had been that terrific run on gold. . . . As soon as the banks reopened, the money started pouring back into the banks. The money poured back into the commercial banks and the gold poured back into the Federal Reserve Banks. It was amazing. I think that here was a new President, been elected by a very large majority, the people had confidence in him, and he did a magnificent job with that "fireside" speech, and he just completely changed the whole psychology.[7]

Roosevelt's contributions to solving the banking crisis, Wyatt added, were "leadership, the courage to sign this proclamation [of closing the banks], and declare a holiday, and that wonderful 'fireside chat'—which I think was a great contribution. He showed more understanding about that than any member of his Brain Trust I saw."[8]

After the banks were reopened, "public psychology" changed dramatically, with more money pouring in than anticipated. Wyatt suggested that "the panic and the bank failures were not the result of the shortage of currency. The banks were just insolvent. Most of the good assets had already been pledged to Federal Reserve Banks or with the

RFC. That was a horrible thing then. When a bank failed, all of its good assets had been pledged to the Federal Reserve Bank."[9]

Ballantine, who downplayed his role in drafting the First Fireside Chat, would write in 1948 that, when the banks opened, confidence was restored. The president "commended the new currency as 'sound currency'" and "expressed assurance that the reopened banks would stand up."[10] And confidence was clearly restored. The amount of currency recovered by the banks was significant and, as a result, new Federal Reserve Bank notes were generally not needed. By the end of March, some $1.2 billion had been returned to the banks, about half of it in gold and gold certificates. By mid-April, some 12,817 banks were fully reopened, with deposits of about $31 billion. By the end of 1933, some 14,440 commercial banks were back in operation, with about $33 billion in operation. Only a handful of banks were put in the hands of conservators. The RFC made loans to banks in the total amount of $260 million and purchased obligations totaling $227 million, a relatively insignificant amount given the overall dimensions of the crisis.[11]

The banking crisis and its devastating impact on the U. S. economy came to a quick and positive end without any of the dire predictions coming to fruition. The quick turn of events was due to Roosevelt's effective persuasion and the people's confidence in the plan to reopen the banks. Equally important was the confidence the people had in the president and the plan forward. Many felt the need to tell Roosevelt how they felt about his radio address, and they did so by communicating directly with the president.

One significant effect of the First Fireside Chat was the sheer size of the audience, estimated at about 40 million radio listeners. Many private citizens wrote Roosevelt, reflecting on his radio speech, commending his message, and promising to do what he asked. For the rhetorical critic, the two thousand letters on file in the Franklin D. Roosevelt Presidential Library are tangible evidence of the speech's effectiveness and impact. An analysis of these letters allows the critic to draw on the themes of the radio address that resonated with his vast audience, assessing the specific rhetorical devices that affected people and actuated many to bring money and gold back to the bank. The letters would clearly show why the nation heeded Roosevelt's request to have confidence in the banking system, thus bringing the crisis to a successful end.

Historian Kennedy estimates that some 450,000 individuals wrote letters to Roosevelt, congratulating him on his fine speech.[12] Many letter writers also added their insight into the speech and the speaker, and many others expounded on the pressure mounting on Roosevelt and asked that he preserve his health. Many letter writers stated their long-standing Republican leaning and their about-face support of Roosevelt once they heard the radio address; others wrote about the inspiration they derived from the First Fireside Chat. Below I discuss a sampling of letters relative to different themes, but many letters cut across several themes.[13]

Instilling Confidence and Generating Support

Many letter writers told Roosevelt how much his radio address brought confidence back, which in turn yielded immediate support for the president and his plan. Myra King Whitson of Houston, a mother "with young mouths to feed, young minds to educate, young fears to quiet," thanked Roosevelt for "your talk last night, when our radio seemed to bring you to us in person—there is deep happiness—a feeling that we have a real share in our government, and that our government is making our welfare its chief concern."[14] For Mrs. Whitson, Roosevelt replaced fear with happiness and made her feel that she had a stake in the government's plan. It is noticeable that Mrs. Whitson used "welfare," the very word Roosevelt used in the address. A letter writer from Wisconsin wrote Roosevelt that "an old friend said to me this morning 'I almost wept during the President's talk last night.'"[15] An Alabama Supreme Court judge opined that "it was an inspiration and I believe will have a most salutary effect and that it will deter ninety per cent of the depositors from making withdrawals when the banks are opened."[16] Though Roosevelt did not directly use deterrence, his subtle threat against hoarding worked.

Jane Covent of Fair Haven, New Jersey, wrote Roosevelt of the hardships many experienced in saving for difficult days ahead only to be told one day that the banks were closed. "One cannot do anything else but worry." But she concluded that the speech over the radio "instilled a new Courage" and thanked Roosevelt for giving her a "new lease of life."[17]

Leonard Ware Jr. of Boston wrote that "you have captured the confidence and devotion of the people in a way that no public man has in our generation."[18] And Mr. Reichardt of Watertown, Wisconsin, wrote on March 14, "It is unfortunate that the radio can not in turn bring to you the great applause of the Wisconsin citizens after they have listened to your radio talks. Your Sunday night's message was wonderful and the citizens are back of you in splendid formation." It is clear that many wished to indicate to Roosevelt that the nation was behind him. Implied in this direct communication is the notion that the people mistrusted politicians in general, but that since the president communicated directly with them, the least they could do was to write directly back to him.

Businessman Mark L. Rothman of Philadelphia took in Roosevelt's entire first week, intimating to the president that, "like all other business men, I have been going about in a daze for the past several months. Your talk, as well as your executive actions since you have taken office, has been a tonic to me as it probably has been to millions of others. . . . If you could talk to the people every week for just fifteen minutes as you did last Sunday, I think that confidence would again be the order to the day."

Benjamin J. Rosenthal of Chicago wrote that "your splendid, forceful address has put new life and confidence in the nation." Thomas A. Raines of Bellwood, Illinois, wrote that the radio speech brought "harmony" to many people, and that "you can rest assured that the way you have started out to protect the honest people that everybody will sacrifice many things in their life to go along with you and help you."

William Pidgeon Jr. of Rochester, New York, wrote to tell the president that his speech "stiffened up my courage and revived a fading hope to new life," and that "your voice and direct appeal to the people regularly would soon be the outstanding fact in our popular and democratic Government." M. B. Jacobsohn of New York City wrote that "your power of voice has had an inclination to restore confidence once more unto the people."

Miss F. I. Hundley of Brooklyn, New York, wrote that the president's "greatest and surest aid will be the radio." She described the heavy burden she and others had carried when "our incomes, savings, homes, everything [was] taken from us and we were helpless to defend ourselves against the forces that seemed bent on our destruction. But now our heads are up again, and our backs will stiffen, too, because you have given us a new hope."

Ben E. Harris of the University of Alabama thought that Roosevelt would appreciate a note from one of the many "forgotten folks," a likely allusion to his "Forgotten Man" speech a year earlier. Roosevelt's construction of his radio audience as comprising many hardworking folks who struggled daily to survive this economic hardship was on the mark. George H. Minnerly of New York City wrote, "Truthfully, I have been greatly worried about my financial status, but after hearing your speech tonight, I must say that my mind is absolutely at ease." J. E. Hooper of Chicago wrote that "your talk last Sunday over the radio was one of the finest steps you could have taken in this present Banking situation. Such moves as that will . . . do more to build up confidence in our Banks and Government then all the Economic Science and Statistics that one could imagine."

Congressman William H. Larrabee of New Palestine, Indiana, expressed how much he appreciated "the splendid address" and added that he was sure "it will do much to allay fear, quiet the unrest and revive confidence among the people of my district." E. Wendell Lamb, a teacher from Bunker Hill, Indiana, wrote that "my history class extends to you their appreciation for your talk," and that "it looks like a mighty fine way to secure a better understanding and cooperation and confidence among your citizens and we hope to be able to listen to you often." Richard Kichen of Omaha, Nebraska, wrote, "Human nature craves personal attention, and undoubtedly you made millions of friends by taking the American people into your confidence. Your speech was most reassuring, the tone of your voice most confident, and your words easy for anyone to understand."

Roosevelt no doubt would have been delighted to read J. Fred Collins, who told the president that his bank in Richmond, Virginia, did not open in the morning and that "if my bank never opens, I know that you have done that which is best and I am with you to the last drop of blood." Trust in Roosevelt was central to the plan to reopen the banks. Perry Morgan, a farmer from Syracuse, New York, wrote to Roosevelt, "If you could see the bright smiles and hear the words spoken of the forgotten man from the Atlantic to the Pacific, from the Great Lakes to the Everglades on March 14th, 1933, of the new deal spoken by one of the greatest Presidents of these United States, it would be the happiest moment of your busy life."

And the Republican Max A. Myerovich of Youngstown, Ohio, assured Roosevelt after hearing his "splendid address last Sunday" that his "organization of five hundred stalwart Republicans are back of you to a man." W. M. Moffett of Detroit, Michigan, "one of the millions of ex-Republicans," thanked Roosevelt for his radio address, adding that "the doubt and uncertainty which dominates so many of us these days were greatly allayed by the inspiration of your words."

Roosevelt's friend Vincent Astor cabled from the yacht *Nourmahal* on March 13 that he "and all the rest of us aboard here have just heard your radio address of confidence to the country and you have made us feel closer to home than our ship could bring us in a good many days." Roosevelt had clearly succeeded in reestablishing confidence in the banks. The people's trust in the president made all the difference in their acceptance of the plan to reopen the banks; the very attempt at a serious plan was good enough for the people. Such sentiments were possible only because of the level of despair many felt.

Instilling Courage and Allaying Fear

For many who listened to the First Fireside Chat, confidence was followed by support in the plan to reopen the banks and consequently confidence in the president, but other letter writers highlighted the degree to which the address instilled courage and hope and allayed fear.

K. R. Kingsbury, president of Standard Oil Company of California, expressed the sentiments of his board in a cable to Roosevelt, congratulating him on "the able and convincing address over the radio . . . which has had a far reaching effect in allaying fear. Also to express our confidence that through your continued firm leadership this country will be returned to prosperity."

A person from Proctor, Minnesota, wrote, "We are taking in all your radio addresses, hear nothing but praise for the fearless actions you are taking, your appeal to the people at 10pm Sunday on the banking situation, hit home, and I don't think any man ever was elected to the high office ever enjoyed such solid support of the people as yourself, and this at a time when the people were ready for any action." This is precisely what Roosevelt hoped to gain from his speech—praise for his fearless actions and strong support from the American people for wide-ranging legislation that would bring an end to the economic turmoil of the previous few years.

Frank J. Cregg, a justice of the New York Supreme Court, wrote Roosevelt from Syracuse that, prior to his speech, there was "a wide divergence of opinion as to whether or not you were going to make good and whether or not you had the confidence of the people," and that "some were frantic and expressed the hope that your message would be such as to allow them to withdraw their life savings from some of the local banks." However, "when your radio talk began everyone seemed to become hypnotized, because there wasn't a word spoken by anyone until you had finished and then as if one voice were speaking all spoke in unison 'We are saved.' The frantic individuals of a few moments before declared that they would leave their money in the banks and that they were not afraid of the future." The First Fireside Chat yielded results in minutes as doom and fear gave way to salvation.

Mrs. Frank Owens, a homesteader from eastern Colorado, wondered if the letter of "an insignificant little farmer's wife" would reach the president. Regardless, she felt the need to tell Roosevelt that, "after hearing your wonderful address last nite, we feel you must be, for the benefit of we poor hardworking people. We sincerely hope so. For we [have] done all we could for you." Desperation turned into hope when Roosevelt's radio talk was taken as caring and sympathetic to the poor and hardworking.

Hiram Neuwoehner wrote, "Your clear, concise radio talk of last night made us realize, for the first time in our lives, the fact that we, an average American family, are really an integral part of our nation—working together we cannot fail. Your talk was wonderful and inspired the maximum confidence." And Nelson T. Niall of New York City opined on March 13, "It did not sound to me like a politician making a speech at all, but sounded like a business man talking, that knew his job + was going to do it regardless of consequences."

F. W. Lovejoy, general manager of Eastman Kodak Company of Rochester, New York, cabled Roosevelt to congratulate him on his "adequate presentation of the banking situation" and suggested that "no matter what his political allegiance may be, every citizen should endorse your frankness and courage and give to your proposed measures." Mr. Lovejoy regretted, however, that one representative to Congress from the Rochester district "was not reported among the band of sincere Republican members to forget politics in this national emergency."

B. Kurlander of Los Angeles, California, described Roosevelt's radio address as an "immortal speech" of "unmistakable words and acts of fearless courage." Miss Evelyn Ehrenworth of Brooklyn, New York, highlighted the wisdom of it all, writing that "even King Solomon couldn't have done anything wiser than President Roosevelt has done."

Father Charles E. Coughlin cabled Colonel M. H. McIntyre, Roosevelt's secretary, the following: "Please offer to our esteemed President my sincerest congratulations for his frank courageous and truthful presentation last night. As far as radio is concerned he is a natural born artist."

Mrs. Betty Seigel took a prophetic approach to her short letter, telling Roosevelt how impressed she was with his radio speech and reminding him of "what the poor late Mayor [of Chicago] Anton Cermak whispered when shot—'the country needs men like you.'"

Francis H. Sisson, president of the American Banks Association, cabled on March 13 to congratulate Roosevelt on "the courageous measures you have taken to stabilize the banking situation in the emergency presented and to assure you of our cordial support in constructive efforts to restore normal banking and business conditions. We believe your strong and reassuring statement to the public Sunday night should greatly aid in the restoration of public confidence upon which recovery must be based."

Mrs. Bertha M. Lindquist of Minneapolis, Minnesota, wrote just minutes after Roosevelt concluded his radio address that "its effect on our little group was just short of being miraculous." She also volunteered that everyone in the group were "all Staunch, hard shelled Republicans." The moment the speech ended, "Mother . . . jumped from her chair saying, 'Isn't he a fine man' and father with tears in his eyes said 'I feel 100% better already.' He had been worrying about his small savings of a lifetime." Mrs. Lindquist concluded her letter by writing that the radio address "could only serve to instill the deepest affection for and confidence in you and your undertakings."[19] Fear turning to hope, in a matter of seconds, was an unprecedented rhetorical success.

C. Richard Suter of Philadelphia wrote on March 12, "As a young Republican who voted against you last November, let me congratulate you on your clear, concise and honest recital of the banking situation and its solution in tonight's broadcast. Never has a modern American President spoken more frankly and sincerely. . . . You spoke to us as a father might speak to his children, giving us courage and hope and a deep sense of security. Every loyal American citizen owes you his support and faith and may I, Mr. President, pledge you mine."

These letter writers, intuitively at least, understood the operative principle of sound economics—confidence in the banking system and confidence in the government, and above all else confidence in the president. Confidence, that illusive commodity and rhetorical currency which Hoover identified but could not produce, was in big supply under Roosevelt.

Faith and Inspiration

Several letter writers adopted a religious tone, identifying both direct and indirect spiritual qualities in Roosevelt's radio speech. Some saw God's hand in Roosevelt's dealings with the banking crisis; others were inspired enough by the radio talk to express faith in the president.

Viola Hazelberger, a high school student from Minneapolis, wrote that she had "gained faith in the banks due to your earnest beliefs. I decided that, as soon as the banks in Minneapolis reopened, I would withdraw my money. When you said that people's money would be safer in the banks than under their mattresses, I decided I'd leave my money just where it is." She concluded by telling the president that she believed that the country "is on the upward grade and . . . that if people will remain calm and composed that the government will pull the United States out of this terrible depression."[20]

Mrs. Louise Hill of Chicago wrote a short and succinct letter, telling Roosevelt that, "while listening to your broadcast Sunday night, our little home seemed a church, our radio the pulpit—and you the preacher. Thank you for the courage and faith you have given us." The hyperbole notwithstanding, Roosevelt benefited from the very seed he planted—faith in him.

Louis H. Jolkovsky of San Antonio wrote, "Your radio speech given last evening was the FINEST proof of American sincerity, and its message conveyed was truly great in the simple language used and direct appeal made to the public." He concluded on a religious note: "Perhaps all these hardships and troubles of the last few years have been forced upon our country so that we could realize another MOSES was needed. To lead our Nation out of the chaos of darkness and discouragement as the MOSES of olden times brought light and happier years to his Nation." Roy V. Crawford of Evanston, Illinois, wrote to Roosevelt via his secretary that "there is no 'Gabriel over the White House.' There is a human in it: Thank providence." A. C. Horn, who did not vote for Roosevelt, wrote that, though he had voted continuously since 1896 and never felt the need to write the president, he was compelled to do so this time because the "radio talk of last night convinced me that if any one can be the Moses to lead us back, Destiny has selected you as that one."

Mrs. A. Keller of Worcester, Massachusetts, titled her letter "A tribute from a Republican." She told the president: "Last Sunday I had many intimations that you were going to visit me. At ten o'clock P. M. I opened the doors of my Radio and admitted you to my home. I listened intently to your most wonderful and inspiring talk, at the close you bade us good night." Her letter ended, like many others, with a hint of divine inspiration: "You have been through the furnace of affliction, saved from an assassin's bullet, all for a reason and that reason is, you are the Moses to lead us out the wilderness." That Moses, a prophet and leader who took his people from bondage to freedom, would be the apt metaphor for Roosevelt's handling of the economic depression and the banking crisis is indicative of the depth of despair and the people's need for salvation. This very metaphor explains why a very straightforward speech devoid of religious allusion was taken as an article of faith in a leader in office for only one week and already adorned with divine inspiration.

B. A. Bonte of Bellevue, Kentucky, inspired by a military metaphor, indicated to Roosevelt that she was "thrilled to hear your voice over the radio. . . . I thought of Nelson's command to his men at Trafalgar, 'England expects every man to do his duty today.' I thought, too, that our President was commanding from his flagship, and shouting through the fog and waves: 'America expects every man to do his duty today.'"

Alberta M. Bell of San Francisco wrote, "There is no radio announcer anywhere who has a better voice than you and I think it would be a great idea if you could and would give a short and brief talk on the current issue of the day over the radio whenever possible. It inspires courage and confidence to hear the truth 'straight from the shoulder.'" And Henry J. Baker of Trenton, New Jersey, wrote, "Your recent radio broadcast message to our people has been a national tonic, meeting universal approval, and has inspired untold confidence in your constructive leadership, so much needed. There seems to be a general feeling and impression that you have accomplished more constructive action during the past ten days, than has been accomplished at any time over the past ten years, and this is from a former Republican, who first of all is an American."

F. L. Brewer, mayor of Madison, Wisconsin, informed Roosevelt that he visited two banks in his town and found "the officials of those banks courageous in their faith in you. On the streets I heard it. In my life time I can remember no time when the American people found such faith in Leadership. And this seems true regardless of party affiliation." D. Hoffman was quite expressive in his letter. He informed Roosevelt that, "in your pre-election speeches, I was almost at the point of hatred towards you, I felt that your talks used uncalled for expressions, and for that reason I did not vote for you. But I can assure you that your Sunday evening talk, has won me over and I am 100% for you hereafter." Mr. Hoffman ended the letter by assuring Roosevelt of being granted "Divine influence and guidance."

Louis C. Emmons of Swarthmore, Pennsylvania, wrote to Roosevelt that a group of die-hard Republicans gathering in Atlantic City cheered for the president after his radio speech, adding that "Herbert Hoover could not have performed any miracle that could have brought forth more applause and favorable comment than your talk."

Many who listened to Roosevelt's First Fireside Chat expected a miracle and were thus inspired by a religious and spiritual message. Though only toward the end of the speech and ever so briefly did Roosevelt talk about salvation and faith, the people saw a God and a Moses in Roosevelt, thus adding a providential hand to the president's actions. Perhaps timing the radio address for Sunday night was suf-ficient for many to assign it a divine purpose.

Rhetorical Assessment

Many letter writers commented on the quality of the radio talk, not-ing its successful rhetorical strength, innovation, precedent setting, intimacy, simplicity, and directness.

Chester E. Burns from Chicago, describing himself as "one of the average citizens," wrote that the Chicago loop is "packed with people, business is being transacted and theirs is a happy and cheerful feeling," all attributed to the "directness" of the radio address with "no foolish words but all good plain talk." He also added that "our country is again united" and that "we are all catching the spirit of your courage and optimism."[21] Harold A. Rohrer, displaying an appreciation for the rhetorical, indicated to Roosevelt that "it seems to me that backed as you are by the confidence of the masses and being the one person to whom they look for deliverance that you can retain that confidence and encourage the people by similar heart to heart talks."

A cashier at the First National Bank of Starbuck, Minnesota, thanked Roosevelt "for the efficient and sensible way you handled this banking situation." Lawrence E. O'Neil of Greensburg, Pennsylvania, wrote "a note of encouragement": "In all of history, in my opinion, we have never had a President to take that honorable position with as many difficulties to surmount as you have. Your talk last evening over the radio regarding the banking situation was wonderful and is appreciated throughout the United States." Richard A. Zimmerman assured Roosevelt that radio addresses such as the one of March 12 would do wonders to get the people to support rules and regulations forwarded by the president, and that "the psychological effect in raising confidence would be of incalculable benefits."

L. C. Curry of Bowling Green, Kentucky, wrote that Roosevelt's discussion of the banking situation "was clear and good, easily understood by the great mass of our citizens." Mr. Curry, an ex-serviceman, informed the president that he had conducted an informal survey of eight hundred high school students and found that 75 percent of them "were able to talk intelligently about its contents."

Hugh R. Robertson wrote that he and his wife "heard your reassuring address to, or more aptly your heart to heart talk with the people of the United States," and that the address "strengthened our faith in you and our confidence in your leadership." Mr. Robertson expressed the opinion of many letter writers in stating, "While what you said was fine and reassuring, the fact that you said it was the important thing—the fact that you, the President of the United States, in the midst of your multitudinous duties and responsibilities, took time to talk directly and frankly to the people of the United States! That was the important and the inspiring thing."

Bernard A. Reinold wrote Roosevelt on behalf of a group of citizens of Czechoslovakian origin that they all "unanimously agreed that the simple words you used, conveyed the message clearly to them in a manner no public address had even done before." Mr. Reinold added that "Shakespeare . . . when he desired to press a point, or purposed a strong scene, used only the simplest words to gain his desired effects," and that the president "must be a close student of Shakespeare." Mrs. Paul H. Russell of Haskell, Oklahoma, wrote, "In your ten minute radio talk Sunday Night you said more than Mr. Hoover did in four years, and although you have culture, aristocratic breeding and wealth you have one priceless gift, that of reaching out to the 'common people' with a deep sympathy and understanding, that goes into their hearts." The pastor of St. Joseph's Rectory in Lebanon, Illinois, congratulated Roosevelt "on Your timely talk to the People of the country, Sunday Night. A talk like that once A Month would be the best tonic you could give to the People, who are confident that you will bring order out of chaos."

Earl L. Peterson, a student at Columbia University, wrote Roosevelt of his skepticism following the closing of all the banks born of the belief that the small depositors would suffer all the losses of the banking failure while the banks "would emerge without any loss at all." Yet the radio address, noted Mr. Peterson, "caused much complimentary discussion because of its intimacy and clarity," and "the interest of the public and not that of the lobbier has been taken into consideration." Mrs. Helen Patterson of Cincinnati, cabled the president, "Your address tonite was a master piece," and "your handling of this vital situation is awe inspiring. Undoubtedly you now have the confidence of the nation."

Similarly, C. C. Passmore of New Orleans wrote, "Your heart-to-heart, sincere, truthful, direct talk with them last Sunday nite over the air just simply revived them and their faith in themselves, as well as endeared you in their hearts." And sister Mary Justitia of Mundelein College in Chicago cabled Roosevelt that "the faculty and students

... pay reverent tribute to you the chief executive of the United States who had the kindness and fellow feeling to set at rest the hearts of your countrymen. Tonight your courage and confidence have enkindled our own. May God grant you guidance and strength and the loyal support of your people."

William Pate of Cleveland wrote, "Your address to the people of the Nation Sunday night over the radio was so simple, so clarifying and so reassuring that all the news and radio talks of the past week faded into insignificance. No one who had the privilege of hearing you could help being thrillingly convinced of the merits of your action."

A letter from Edward W. Pau of the House of Representatives must have thrilled the president. The congressman wrote that Roosevelt's radio address "was perfect," and that it reminded him of "one of the powerful deliverances of Woodrow Wilson during the war." Mr. Hutchinson of the New York Athletic Club of New York City, who claimed to know Roosevelt personally, congratulated him on "the elementary method of presentation you followed last night. Granted your confidence in return for theirs, they will stand behind you solidly." Mr. Hutchinson offered, "My very dear old friend, you have the opportunity of the Ages to do the most good ever done by any President or Sovereign since Time began: and you will go down in History as *the* outstanding Chief Executive of all Time."

Mrs. Lourie G. Barry of Tulsa, Oklahoma, wrote prophetically that "to be addressed by our President in phrases of homely meaning, neighborly words, as friend to friend, even in words of anxious solicitation for our welfare, coming straight from the heart, was a startling experience in view of past events. It was a momentous occasion—history alone can record its importance." She concluded by stating that the president "restored American democracy" and, echoing Lincoln, that "the ideals and sacrifices of our forefathers are again justified, and this nation is, with you at the helm, a government for the people." The novelty of Roosevelt's simple speaking style, the likes of which people were not used to hearing from their presidents, was a significant reason for the success of the radio address, as many indicated. Letter writers also commented on his heart-to-heart talk, reflecting on the direct and honest account of the banking situation Roosevelt outlined.

Dr. Edward A. Mallon of Philadelphia congratulated Roosevelt on his "wonderful, clear, quiet, concise, logical talk which you gave on Sunday evening. It was as if an old, tried and true friend had called on a Sunday evening and had talked, advised, counseled, and said adieu. I shall be back gain. I have only praise for you." Claude B. Norris of Youngtown, Ohio, wrote, "Your radio address last night was wonderful. It seemed as if a good neighbor had dropped in to explain something that was giving us much concern."

David I. Kaplan of New York City wrote that the "statement on the radio on the banking situation was doubly effective because of its utter simplicity. Even the children went to bed happier for having heard it. . . . In spirit and in emotion you were present in every home and at every hearth, gathered with the rest of the family, telling us things that were assuring and comforting." And several individuals from St. Louis jointly told Roosevelt that "any one who 'listened in' could not but feel the sincerity of your words, and the logic of your explanation. Your far-sightedness in a direct communication to the citizens of our Republic is an answer to doubt, and a word of confidence to America's." These writers added, "To know that the chief executive is alive to the conditions that confront us all, is somewhat of a relief to the average citizen. Heretofore the direct contact was unknown, but your talk last nite we believe has brought to Americans the fact that the 'President' is just an average American, with the same thoughts and hopes that we all have."

Mrs. Joseph D. Johns of Boerne, Texas, wrote, "Your little talk on Sunday evening tied some heart strings that won't be easily broken. It gave us a tangible contact and feeling that we are being treated as individuals for consideration and not just 'mass production.'" Similarly, F. W. Meyers of Iowa City wrote that "it was cosy and friendly and cheery to have you with us last night. We invited some friends in 'to meet the President,' not forgetting to place an easy chair by the fireplace for the guest of honor, and when your voice came, so clear and vibrant and confident, we had but to close our eyes to see you sitting there with us, talking things over in friendly fashion." James A. Green of Cincinnati, wrote, "You have a marvelous radio voice, distinct and clear. It almost seemed the other night . . . that you were across the room from me. A great many friends have said the same thing. . . . As for the message itself, it was clear, forcible and direct—a wonderful thing for the President of the United States to talk to the people as you talked to them."

Mr. and Mrs. F. B. Graham of Dubuque, Iowa, wrote Roosevelt that they appreciated him for honoring "every home with a personal visit last night," for coming "into our living-room in a kindly neighborly way and in simple words explain[ing] the great things he had done so that all of us unfamiliar with the technicalities might understand. When his voice died away we realized our 'friend' had gone home again but left us his courage, his faith and absolute confidence." The Grahams also told Roosevelt that, as long as he talks to the people, "there is not one thing you cannot accomplish," and that "Congress and other law-makers will find themselves puny interference when you have but to turn to the Radio and enter our home a welcome and revered guest." The Grahams continued, telling Roosevelt that "of all precedents you have shattered is the theory that a man must come from the lowly to understand the needs of the common people. We love you for that perception that could come from a great unselfish heart." Finally, the Grahams expressed the opinion of many: "Since March 4th . . . we knew we were not fighting alone. We have a LEADER at last." Hoover was probably disturbed to learn how easily Roosevelt turned the tide and how quickly he restored confidence and made himself a friend and inspiration to so many Americans.

Carl F. Geigand of Buffalo, New York, wrote about the "most enlightening radio address last evening," adding that "we are, all of us, bound to have confidence in your administration if, by recourse to the radio, you will take us into your confidence from time to time. By the same instrument, influences, adverse to your wise legislative policies, can be brought into proper alignment since the power of public opinion will be thrown in the balance." Though Mr. Geigand's letter focuses on the confidence Roosevelt instilled in the nation, he insightfully rationalized it in terms of successful public influence, getting close to figuring out Roosevelt's rhetorical strategy.

Emile Grever of Cincinnati wrote that he had never "heard a speech come over the air so distinctly, so splendidly enunciated and in words so well chosen for the average hearer. Not a word was lost. There was something intimate about it, something that made one feel that his best friend was talking." Roosevelt probably appreciated greatly the added statement about his own hero: "In a New York interview yesterday, Speaker Rainey said, 'The President is going to be a second Woodrow Wilson.' May I not remind him that even today there are greater men than Ceasar; which does not dim the luster of Ceasar's name." For Roosevelt to be equated with his hero, President Wilson, was quite an accomplishment.

R. J. Dunham of Chicago cabled that "people here have all been electrified with his radio talk," and that "indications are the country today is with him more than ever." T. B. Daves of Mobile, Alabama, congratulated Roosevelt on his radio talk, suggesting that "occasional heart to heart talks with your people, like the one of Sunday night, will tend to bring you closer to them and will inspire the utmost confidence in your leadership." And a struggling young author from Topeka, Kansas, wrote that in his opinion the speech concerning the banking situation "went the Gettysburg address of Lincoln's one better." Roosevelt was now on par with Woodrow Wilson's oratory and Abraham Lincoln's hallmark speech.

Dr. Bernard Meyer, an economics professor at the College of the City of New York, expressed his "unqualified appreciation of your informal methods of reaching the people directly regarding their best economic welfare." The professor also opined that "the confidence which you inspire, is an indispensable pre-requisite to the success of any economic program for the rescue of your country, from predatory finance on the one hand and irrational radicalism on the other." The economics theorist was well matched by a practical banker, Jeremiah D. Maguire of the Federation Bank and Trust Company of New York City, who congratulated Roosevelt "on the very lucid, instructive and timely expression made by you in your radio talk last evening." Mr. Maguire also indicated to the president that the bank "came through the test of the last week in good shape, was given its license in the first batch of licenses issued and is rolling along in a normal fashion endeavoring to serve the purpose which I know was your intent when you first undertook the reopening programme."

Nathan Miller of Pittsburgh wrote, "I have just heard your plain and frank radio message to the American people on the banking situation. I hope that this unprecedented innovation will prove to be of a permanent institution whereby the condition of the ship of State will be brought to us direct from you." Mr. Miller also suggested that "Huey Long and other demagogues may succeed for a while to becloud the issues by spreading a blanket of mist and fog on the political horizon, but it will soon vanish and dissipate under the pitiless publicity of your direct plain speech to us at the appropriate moment."

Archie A. Anderson of Leachville, Arkansas, wrote: "When you went on the air recently and took the American people into your confidence on the banking question you did an unprecedented thing for a President. In my humble opinion it was the finest thing a President ever did. ... You called us 'friends' over the air and I hope you will not consider me presumptions when I sign myself, Your Friend."

Anthony Morse from Jacksonville, Florida, and a Roosevelt friend from Warm Springs, Georgia, wrote that "your Bank talk Sunday week was greatly appreciated by the People of Jacksonville, not only for its information, but largely that you are the first President in many generations who has taken the Public into their confidence in the administration of their affairs." Brian Miller of Philadelphia took an imaginary approach in his letter. He thanked the president for his "visit at 10 o'clock Sunday night. I can see you seated in the big armchair in my living room, pipe in mouth and talking on the crisis that confronts us all, telling me in words that I could understand what you had done and the reasons for your action." This imaginative depiction has since become the epitome of the fireside chat as an intimate exchange between the president and the people.

Henry C. Zeller of Buffalo took a more comprehensive view of the first week in his letter to Roosevelt: "Your Banking act, Economy measure and Beer bill, all excellent and necessary measures toward return of prosperity, that at once brought immeasurable relief thruout the country and splendid co-operation from everyone. . . . Then, too, your last Sunday's radio talk was forceful, yet in language easily understood by your vast audience and very favorably commended on by everybody." John Watson of Reiffton, Pennsylvania, took an interesting approach not witnessed in other letters: "This dictator talk gives me the wearies. Anyhow, I'd rather have an honest man tell me what to do, and what not to do, than be up in the air all the time."

Joseph W. Homer of Brookline, Massachusetts, wrote immediately after listening to Roosevelt's "straightforward, reassuring talk on banks and banking" that, though he did not vote for the president, he had been "thrilled and inspired by the promptness, decisiveness, effectiveness and courtesy with which you have wielded 'the big stick' during past week."

Prewitt B. Turner complemented Roosevelt on his "masterful" radio talk, displaying his understanding of the president's overall rhetorical plan: "You are an outstanding salesman, and that's very important. Your approach (inaugural speech) and demonstration (bank holiday) was followed by a psychological and dynamic close (your radio explanation). You've sold yourself and policies to your countrymen, signed them on the dotted line and progress on a sound basis will result." Mr. Turner succinctly summarized the entire first week in office as one rhetorical package.

Indeed, Roosevelt's penchant for doing things the dramatic way always helped him. He was the first to attend a party convention, breaking with the long-standing tradition of waiting for party officials to come to the presidential candidate's home to inform him of the party nomination; he was the first to fly to a convention; and now, though not the first president to speak through the radio, he spoke to the people like no president before him. The novelty of it all was a significant reason for his success, and the people took notice of the unprecedented talk, its simplicity and directness, and its ability to generate confidence and support.

Many letter writers who congratulated Roosevelt on his First Fireside Chat also advised him to continue to address the nation via the radio. One letter writer, M. M. Gubin of Aberdeen, North Dakota, representing the opinions of many, stated that "I earnestly hope that President Roosevelt will make a weekly talk to the people of the United States. He talks in language all can understand and in a spirit that all appreciate. He can ELIMINATE politics and secure the loyal support of all right-thinking Americans by such talks as that given Sunday. We will never solve America's problems by listening to Amos and Andy or solving jig-saw puzzles. If the President will give a weekly talk, all America will be listening in in a short time." Many also asked that the president take care of his health, given his hard work and the many challenges ahead.

Collectively this extensive sample of letters written in reaction to the First Fireside Chat points to several themes that resonated with the public: courage, confidence, friendship, closeness/proximity of the people to their president, appreciation for the president's closeness to the people, and restoration of people's faith in their government. Roosevelt was complimented for his direct, intimate, and honest speech. Many letter writers noted the religious, moral, and inspirational qualities of Roosevelt's First Fireside Chat even though the president had very little to say that can be construed as religious. Roosevelt did, however, talk about his faith in the people, and the people returned that faith tenfold, looking up to him as a leader of a great crusade. Roosevelt's rhetoric made him the focal point of the crisis at hand. And though many letters display naïve patriotism and simplicity of sentiment toward the nation's leader, the letters are well within the discursive practices of the period when trust in the government and its leaders was practiced and expected. Religion was clearly an important marker for ordinary citizens and a yardstick for their relationship with the polity in general and the president in particular.

On Roosevelt's Style and Delivery

Roosevelt's language, style, and delivery were all essential for his effective radio address, and the letter writers who responded to him indicated as much, highlighting his clarity, directness, and simplicity of speaking.

Benjamin J. Rosenthal of Chicago wrote that he heard a person say "the President put some 'pep' in me last night in his talk. That was fine sales talk. I am going out now to do business." Hugh R. Robertson of San Antonio, Texas, wrote: "Last night my wife and I heard your reassuring address, or more aptly your heart to heart talk with the people of the United States, and we both felt the bracing effect of it, as did thousands of others." Earl L. Peterson of Brooklyn, New York, wrote, "Your radio speech . . . has caused much complimentary discussion because of its intimacy and clarity." And William Pidgeon of Rochester, New York, who appreciated the president's message, wrote that his "voice and direct appeal to the people regularly would soon be the outstanding fact in our popular and democratic Government."

W. H. Perry of Phoenix, Arizona, wrote that the radio address, "couched in words of one syllable . . . was easily understood by anyone." William Pate of Cleveland, Ohio, wrote that the address "was so simple, so clarifying and so reassuring that all the news and radio talks of the past week faded into insignificance." Mrs. Lourie C. Barry of Tulsa appreciated being "addressed by our President in phrases of homely meaning, neighborly words, as friend to friend, even in words of anxious solicitation for our welfare, coming straight from the heart." Louis H. Jolkovsky of Houston wrote that the radio speech "was the FINEST proof of American sincerity, and its message conveyed was truly great in the simple language need and direct appeal made to the public." And F. W. Meyers of Iowa City told the president that, "when your voice came, so clear and vibrant and confident, we had but to close our eyes to see you sitting there with us, talking things over in friendly fashion."

James A. Green of Cincinnati wrote, "You have a marvelous radio voice, distinct, and clear." Edmond Grever, also of Cincinnati, wrote that he never "heard a speech come over the air so distinctly, so splendidly enunciated and in words so well chosen for the average hearer." Alberta M. Bell of San Francisco wrote that "there is no radio announcer anywhere who has a better voice than you." An anonymous letter writer opined that "there is that something in your voice conveying absolute sincerity." Edward A. Mallon of Philadelphia congratulated Roosevelt on his "wonderful, clear, quiet, concise, logical talk." D. J. Matlack of Clearwater, Florida, wrote, "In our childhood days, my father would read to us from the paper and my sister would remark, after he had finished the article: 'Now papa tell us about it.' You did and made it clear to everyone." Roosevelt took the mantle of the nation's father, explaining to his children the events of the day.

C. G. Adams of Baldwin, Long Island, wrote that, "from the moment that you first cast into the troubled maelstrom of our American life that spiritual vision of 'the forgotten man' I have felt that you understood as no other in your position has done the soul of the people." And L. M. Tracey of San Francisco commented on the essence of political rhetoric: "We know from History that the voice of the commanding General coming to the ears of the rank and file of the Army has many times turned the course of famous battles in warfare of the past, and if you will keep that splendid voice of yours before the American people on matters of common interest, I cannot see how you can fail in your present assignment."

The most frequent word clusters found in many letters to Roosevelt illustrate just how the speech resonated with the American people. Words such as "friend," "neighbor," "heart-to-heart," "faith," "Moses," "confidence," "leadership," "inspired," "fearless," and "reassuring" speak volumes about the speech and the speaker. The letter writers attributed to the speaker and his speech some of the very words used in the speech. Additionally, these frequently used attributes represent the degree to which the focal point of the listeners was on Roosevelt, his persona, approach, sympathy, skills, and inspiration. Here lie the reasons the First Fireside Chat was such an effective speech: It resonated so well with the people's sentiments and the solution people were hoping for that it yielded the results Roosevelt sought. The rhetorical and political objectives all aligned to secure the effects sought.

The Press Reaction

The press was equally impressed with Roosevelt's first week in office and particularly with his First Fireside Chat. Confidence in the ability of the banks to reopen without additional hoarding surfaced even before this address. A headline from March 10 read, "Sound D.C. banks to reopen Tuesday," and a March 11 headline stated, "New York banks ready to open." A March 12 headline in the *Washington Herald* stated, "Institutions in 12 Reserve Cities to Reopen Tomorrow." A smaller headline on the same page stated, "Boston Banks get Flood of checks," and the short article explained that thousands of checks had been processed, citing the resumption of some normalcy. Another March 12 headline read, "Virginia to hasten opening of banks."[22] The *New York Times* announced on March 12 that "brokers expect brisk trading when Exchanges Reopen."

After the broadcast of the First Fireside Chat, the *Wall Street Journal* published on March 13 that Roosevelt's first week in office "marked an end to three years of a nation's drifting from bad to worse, an end to helpless acceptance of a malign fate which half-hearted, half-way measures gave hope to averting.... For an explanation of the incredible change which has come over the face of things here in the United States in a single week we must look to the fact that the new administration in Washington has superbly risen to the occasion."[23]

In London, the *Times* reported on March 13 on the "return of hoarded gold," noting that the Federal Reserve Bank saw the return of some $108,000,000 in gold, and that in Chicago alone some "$9,000,000 in gold was taken at the reserve bank." The *Christian Science Monitor* reported on March 13, "Large City Banks Reopen with Others To Follow For Two Successive Days." The same newspaper assessed Roosevelt's first week in office as "probably without parallel in the history of markets. ... Happily the week ended with every indication that before long the world will be back to market normality." The *Wall Street Journal* front page headline on March 14 read, "Bank Crisis Passes: U.S. Credit Comes Next." A smaller headline on the same page stated, "Confidence Back as Banks Reopen." On the same day, the *Christian Science Monitor*'s headline read, "Torrent of Gold Overflows Banks of Chicago area."

Several months after the banking crisis had subsided, an essay in *Atlantic Monthly* took the unconventional approach of conversing with the president: "Your forgotten man has come a long way since last

November.... He has come ... an even longer way since March 4." The essay continued with a plea for forgiveness since the people failed to do justice to their president. Now the people had to tell the president several things: "What you told us from the beginning was truth," and "You have taken us into a relationship in which we can profoundly believe, and we must try to keep our side of it not less sensitive, not less candid, than you seem to be keeping yours." The essay concluded: "We give you back, Mr. President, syllable for syllable, the last words which you have spoken directly to and for us before this writing: 'In the present spirit of mutual confidence and mutual encouragement *we go forward.*'"[24] The "forgotten man" of the 1932 radio address was forgotten no longer; the people remembered. These two radio addresses were thus tied into one continuous and organic relationship between the nation's leader and the people.

As one of Roosevelt's most important and successful public addresses, the First Fireside Chat cannot be appreciated without configuring the immediate rhetorical text—the first week in office. This rhetorical text commenced with a tremendously successful inaugural address followed by closing the banks, engaging the press, sending messages to Congress and to the public, and getting the Emergency Banking Act passed. The rhetorical text also carried the implied comparison with Roosevelt's immediate predecessor in the White House.

From the moment of being sworn into office, the president constructed the image of an administration ready to roll up its sleeves and take action. The actions of the first week were largely rhetorical, that is, they were mere words. But the words were crucial, for they sought to instill hope, confidence, and faith in the new president and his promise to bring salvation to the nation. The first week was packed with so many words that surely the public could not escape the comparison with Hoover's lengthy silence over his final months in office. From passivity to action, the public now heard a president who spoke differently and emphatically, offered commonsense wisdom, castigated those who needed castigating, and offered faith and friendship to the many who suffered under economic stress.

The first week concluded with the radio address that was to end the economic turmoil brought by the banking crisis of the past few months and the economic depression of the past few years. The address was successful primarily because it was direct, even blunt, and its speaker minced no words. The president displayed his trust in the people, understood their suffering, and assured them that things would get better. He also asked them to do the right thing by leaving money and currency in the banks, and even bring back currency and gold hoarded earlier. The president's faith in the people was returned literally in gold.

Roosevelt's radio address ushered in a new era and a new relationship between the president and the American people, using this fireside chat and the many more to come to expand "the possibilities of democracy when a leader addresses the masses with messages that actually have something to say." In so doing, Roosevelt "moved this epistolary dialogue to the larger public conversation he conducted with the people through his speeches and radio addresses."[25] The First Fireside Chat succeeded on two levels. On one level, it reassured the American people that the banking system was sound and that, once reopened, most banks were solvent; it prevented additional hoarding of currency and gold; and it convinced many to redeposit currency and gold in the banks, reversing the course of events that brought the United States to near financial collapse. On another level, it introduced a mode of communication between the president and the people that was unique, intimate, and effective. Roosevelt found a way to speak to the people directly and frame his talk as a friendly chat. In so doing, Roosevelt carved a new presidential persona that allowed for a different kind of politics, the kind that solicited the people's support over a wide range of political issues. The radio medium entered a new constellation of the relationship between the president, the legislature, and the people. There would be no match to Roosevelt's mastery of a communication medium for effective politics until Ronald Reagan showed politicians his mastery of the television medium decades later.

Saving Capitalism

The First Fireside Chat must be appreciated for the complexity of its construction. Crafting the proper rhetorical appeal is never an easy task, and it is doubly challenging during a crisis. In the context of a lengthy interregnum between Hoover and Roosevelt, a reluctant outgoing president and a strategic president-elect would look at the banking crisis similarly but handle its resolution differently. The banking crisis would bring the nation near financial collapse before Roosevelt entered the White House as a savior who in one week both closed and reopened the banks. The president and the new administration engaged in highly dramatic and symbolic acts as persuasive tools of governance, all calculated to bring the banking crisis to a quick end. The inaugural address of March 4 and the First Fireside Chat of March 12 bookended a most intense week in American history in which the president showcased his tremendous rhetorical skills as tools of effective politics.

The First Fireside Chat yielded the results Roosevelt sought, and his first week in office ended on a high note. The nation took stock of the president's activities, both symbolic and material. The banking crisis came to an end on the morning of March 13, 1933, when banks opened again as Roosevelt promised. Hoarding did not resume; in fact, many Americans brought back currency and gold. In a matter of days, banks began to feel secure and solvency resumed quickly.

The nation was grateful, and many citizens wrote to the president, displaying a keen understanding of the complexity of the situation and the skills required for its resolution. Joseph Warren Homer of Brookline, Massachusetts, wrote to the president on March 12, immediately after listening to his radio address. His letter reflects a comprehensive understanding of Roosevelt's approach to solving the banking crisis. "I have just been listening to your simple, straight-forward, reassuring talk on the banks and banking. I have been thrilled and inspired by the promptness, decisiveness, effectiveness and courtesy with which you have wielded 'the big stick' during the past week. I did not vote for you because, altho independent, my proclivities during the past ten years have been Republican and it seemed to me to be impolitic to 'swap horses in the middle of the stream.'" Mr. Homer then concluded with, "I am writing this as one of those whom I heard you address last fall as 'The Forgotten man.'" The radio address several months earlier was still echoing in the public sphere and contextualizing for many, including many Republicans, the success of Roosevelt's appeal. A simple and direct speaking style aiding the straightforward message was all Roosevelt needed to appeal to most Americans, who absorbed every word, every syllable and intonation. They also understood the request the president made of them, and they put his appeals in the larger rhetorical context that began several months earlier with another successful radio address.

The enormity of Roosevelt's rhetorical success is aptly expressed in a recent essay by Jonathan Alter in *Newsweek:* "In the days following his 'fear itself' Inaugural and first 'Fireside Chat,' the same citizens who had lined up the month before to withdraw their last savings from the bank (and stuff it under the mattress or tape it to their chests) lined up to redeposit patriotically. This astounding act of ebullient leadership marked the 'defining moment' of modern American politics, when Roosevelt saved both capitalism and democracy within a few weeks."[1] The banking crisis was brought to an abrupt end by the new president, who was taken by the nation as a savior. His appeal to the people yielded immediate results and, though similar contexts in Europe carried ominous signs, Roosevelt kept the political system intact. The

First Fireside Chat was a masterful stroke, and the American people appreciated their leader's trust in them; they gave him their complete trust in return.

The Holdovers Leave

Roosevelt would give twenty-six more fireside chats over his twelve years in office, each focusing on a specific topic of importance. He would also give many more radio addresses not designated as fireside chats. All fireside chats would be highly anticipated and become an integral part of Roosevelt's presidential rhetoric.

Arthur B. Ballantine, the Hoover holdover who more than anyone else was key to the reopening of the banks, who organized the essential legislative efforts of Roosevelt's first week in office and drafted the First Fireside Chat, carried on until the banking crisis was over. Then, after repeated requests, he left the Roosevelt administration. Roosevelt appreciated Ballantine's work so much that he initially did not relieve him of his duties. As early as March 17, only a few days after the First Fireside Chat, Ballantine wrote Roosevelt to make clear that he wished to leave the administration as soon as possible. Roosevelt's reply cited how much "Mr. Woodin and I deeply appreciate all that you have done."[2] On April 14, Ballantine met Roosevelt and indicated to the president that "not much progress seemed to have been made about relieving me from my position." Ballantine also indicated to Roosevelt his belief that "a Republican in this position as a holdover could not give to the Secretary by any means the full assistance he required, and that it would be very much better for the Secretary to have a Democrat in my place."[3] In his last letter to Ballantine upon his departure, Roosevelt stated, "It is a real pleasure to express my great appreciation of the high character of your service to the Government and to the country."[4] Ballantine was succeeded on May 15 by Dean Acheson as the new undersecretary of the treasury.

In *The Ghost Talks*, Charles Michelson stated that Woodin had to take an authoritative tone with the Hoover holdovers, whose philosophy was "poles apart from the fiscal policies of the Roosevelt administration," and that the holdovers had to conform to the new administration's policies. Upon reading this account, Ballantine replied that Michelson was distorting history and added that "on questions of financial policy, Mr. Woodin did not differ at all with us at the Treasury. Far from using a note of authority and insisting that we holdovers come to heel, he took and followed advice with the utmost readiness and fidelity, gladly taking full advantage of the Treasury thought represented by us 'holdovers.'"[5]

Michelson got it wrong again. On June 14, Secretary of the Treasury Woodin wrote Ballantine a private letter. He indicated to Ballantine that he had tried to write this letter some sixteen times but that all were "consigned . . . to the wastepaper basket, because all dictionaries of the English language that I possess do not some way or another seem to have the proper words with which to express my thoughts." Woodin continued: "The greatest rainbow of the whole affair here since March 4th was learning to know, admire and conceive great affection for Arthur Ballantine. You are certainly a patriot if there ever was one, and I shall never forget how nobly you stood by the ship and very often prevented me from making some of those high dives to which I am afraid I am somewhat prone, which might have ended up in a lot of broken bones."[6]

Though Roosevelt expressed great appreciation for the Hoover holdovers, especially Ballantine and Awalt, the press, not fully aware of the extent of the help these individuals forwarded, was less generous. One newspaper article wrote that "the Roosevelt Administration intends to dispense with the services of F. G. Awalt, acting comptroller of the currency, and A. A. Ballantine, under secretary of the Treasury as soon as possible," and that "their handling of the Detroit banking situation and other aggravated fiscal mix-ups over the country has expedited the decision. In addition, the Roosevelt Administration feels that it can entrust such delicate jobs only to persons in whose judgment it has extreme confidence." Finally, the newspaper article specifically stated that Ballantine's advice during the banking failure in Detroit was faulty and that "he should be relieved as soon as possible."[7]

This was a slap in the face to the person who did more than most to save the banks. Notwithstanding Roosevelt's attempt to keep Ballantine as treasury undersecretary as long as possible, the press account clearly indicates that someone was looking for a convenient scapegoat. As for the motive for this press account, Ballantine suggests that several officials of the Hoover Treasury, including the ex-treasury secretary Ogden Mills, stayed on to lend a hand "until the New Dealers became for some reason fearful about that never-acknowledged help" of some of Hoover's top officials.[8]

The need for a scapegoat may also have been related to a grand jury investigation of the banking failure in Detroit. The specific accusation was that closing the Guardian Detroit Union group and the First National Banks "was a plot by 'Wall Street and the Morgan Group' to 'get Henry Ford' through collusion with Federal officials."[9] However, in a related twist of events, the now acting treasury secretary, Dean Acheson (following Woodin's death only a few months into the Roosevelt administration), rejected requests by a Detroit federal court to hand over documents related to the banking failure in that city and force a Treasury official to testify. The reason for this refusal, cited Acheson, was in the potential hampering of Treasury duties in Detroit and elsewhere. Acheson also cited the fact that ex-Treasury officials, including Ballantine, were no longer Treasury employees and thus could not be forced to testify, and that agents of the comptroller of the currency were not Treasury officials but paid out of "a special fund derived from assessment on the national banks."[10] Indeed, the Roosevelt administration had much to thank Ballantine and other Hoover holdovers for and likely did not wish to see them go through unnecessary litigation.

In a letter to Roy Chapin, Hoover's secretary of commerce who accompanied Ballantine on that fateful visit to Detroit in February, Ballantine stated that "what was done in the crisis itself"—meaning the measures taken to stop the run on the banks, the First Fireside Chat, the reopening of the banks and reestablishment of sound banking—were all "shaped by the forces that continued and the advisors whom they [the Roosevelt administration] called in."[11] This is all true.

As for the banking crisis and the degree to which either Hoover or Roosevelt was responsible for its exacerbation, much has been written about the impasse between the two protagonists. Yet any assessment about what would have happened had Roosevelt acceded to Hoover's requests for help or Hoover acted on his own without the blessing of the president-elect must take into consideration two aspects: the political and the rhetorical. Politically, Roosevelt could not have agreed to Hoover's repeated requests for statements of confidence, for they would literally end the very program—the New Deal—that propelled Roosevelt to the presidency. Neither could Roosevelt agree to issue statements denying his plan for a "sound money" when in fact he planned to devalue the dollar and get the United States off the gold standard. Rhetorically, Hoover was at a clear disadvantage for not realizing that the economic crisis and especially the banking crisis required a hefty dose of rhetorical measures. Even though Hoover talked about the need to restore confidence, he did not develop the rhetoric that could articulate it. Roosevelt was a master rhetorician who constructed the very advantage of entering the White House at the moment when the crisis was most acute and the public most receptive to any solution a president might propose. The First Fireside Chat secured the public's overwhelming support in the plan to reopen the banks.

The banks were saved, and the nation survived the greatest threat to its financial and economic foundations, largely on the basis of a plan developed in the Hoover administration and put into effect by Hoover holdovers. Ballantine would suggest some fifteen years later that "it is hard to see that such a speech [Roosevelt's First Fireside Chat] could not have been made with equal effect before closing of the banks or that final remedial steps could not have taken in time for avoidance of that calamity."[12] To such a claim one can reply that Hoover could not have delivered such an effective speech despite the availability of outstanding speechwriters such as Ballantine. Hoover was either unable or unwilling to master the leadership necessary to bring Congress to pass important legislation such as the Emergency Banking Act, on which the entire reopening of the banks was made possible. Hoover could not even muster the courage to allow the 1917 Trading with the Enemy Act to serve as the legal precedent for closing all banks. Neither did Hoover possess the oratorical skills to speak clearly and effectively to the nation.

Hoover was also unwilling to realize the heavy price the United States paid for keeping itself on the gold standard, making American products too expensive just at the moment when consumption was essential for renewing productivity and employment. To expect Roosevelt to disavow any intention to get the United States off the gold standard was a narrow-minded approach to the economic crisis and specifically the run on the banks. Hoover could not even agree on the best course of action and found himself disagreeing with his own Treasury officials. Roosevelt took a broader view of the banking crisis, noting the fairly strong stock market and the strength of the dollar despite the depletion of gold reserves. Roosevelt also possessed a better view of the rhetorical forces of economic behavior, understanding, perhaps intuitively, that faith had a major role to play in the nation's economy and constructing his rhetoric accordingly. The claim that Roosevelt did not have a solution, even days prior to his inauguration,[13] is true only insofar as one limits such a solution to technical measures. But Roosevelt's solution was primarily rhetorical. Closing the banks or, more accurately, reaffirming the closure of banks already decided by many state governors was a rhetorical act, as were most measures taken during the first week in office. Roosevelt said as much during a discussion of the Thomas Amendment when he asked rhetorically how he knew that a $10 bill was "any good." His reply: "The fact that I think it is, makes it good."[14] In short, banking credibility is all about confidence in the banking system. Perhaps by happenstance, as suggested by Roosevelt biographer Freidel, or perhaps by keen observation, the crisis at hand was more psychological than real.[15]

Final Thoughts

Much has been gleaned from the many letters private citizens wrote their president in response to the First Fireside Chat. One final letter captures its essence beautifully. Marie Barrell of New York City situated Roosevelt's radio address in the larger historical context, illustrating insightfully how Roosevelt restored faith in the banks and in the nation's economy:

Last night I was one of your millions of eager listeners. How simple, human, straightforward and honest you were! What a note of high courage rang in your voice! How you heartened us and warmed us toward you, our magnificent intrepid President!

What a renewal of faith you are kindling in a government that has been debased; what hope you are bringing to a people who have been betrayed and deceived by fearful and small-minded politicians, by unscrupulous and avaricious financiers and big business men!

Since the War we have sunk deeper and deeper into the ignominious morass of crass greed, corrupt politics, confused thinking and gross materialism. We seemed to have lost our national soul. Thoughtful men and women were filled with shame and sorrow at our great departure from the simple truths. They viewed with growing apprehension the body politic and the economic set-up.

We cried for a Leader. And out of all this confusion, fear, nay impending disaster—you have come to us, splendidly, fearless, crystal-clear in your thinking, decisive and direct in action! Now we have a rallying point. Your dauntlessness and faith are contagious.

Last Saturday, your inaugural address stirred us profoundly. We recognized the deeply passionate note of the crusader. We have been watching with breathless interest and admiration your fearless and intelligent actions during your first seven days—these are already history—we, who had witnessed nothing but delay, inactivity and hedging for four long years. Nero fiddled while Rome burned!

Last evening you talked to us, your troubled people. How deeply you endeared yourself to us, because of your directness, warm sympathy and profound understanding of our heartbreaking problems.

Surely, the voice of the people was the voice of God, last November—and you have already done so much to prove this. As one of your predecessors wrote: 'It is rarely that the public sentiment decides immorally or unwisely.'

God bless you and keep you in good health and unharmed for the onerous, but what must be soul satisfying leadership, of us—your people.

Yours in deep admiration.

This letter is written from the depths of despair, expressing relief that the new president was courageous and that he would restore the nation's faith and confidence in the government and the economy. The letter attributes morality and divine inspiration to Roosevelt in contrast to the corrupt practices of the previous administration. The letter echoes Roosevelt's rhetoric of his first week in office, accepting his request not to fear fear and to abide by the simple truths. Finally, the letter expresses admiration for the president for endearing himself to the people with the simple and warm rhetoric of his radio talk.

Marie Barrel captured the nation's sentiments but also Roosevelt's innate leadership and rhetorical skills. His First Fireside Chat was contextualized poetically to yield an astute understanding of a nation yearning for a courageous leader who would restore faith in the body politic. Roosevelt, according to Barrel, possessed a solid understanding of the political and historical forces as well as insights into how to appeal to human nature by restoring faith and confidence—this was the essence of his rhetorical skills. In only seven days in office Roosevelt did just that, commencing his presidency with a powerful appeal to ban fear and ending with a powerful speech to have faith in his plan to reopen the banks.

On March 13, while Congress was debating the economic bill, Roosevelt recommended an immediate modification of the Volstead Act, proposing to legalize the manufacture and sale of beer and light wines, literally ending Prohibition.[16] Democrats praised the move and quickly passed the legislation on the economic bill on March 15, and the beer bill followed the next day. Roosevelt, the master of rhetoric and timing, obviated the nation's heavy concern over the economy and banking with the lightness of alcohol. The recovery was clearly under way.

Notes

Address of President Roosevelt by Radio, March 12, 1933

1. Franklin D. Roosevelt, Fireside Chat, Number One, "The Banking Crisis," March 12, 1933, Master Speech File, No. 616a, Franklin D. Roosevelt Library. I have used the authenticated version of the speech as it appears in the Speechbank web site, www.americanrhetoric.com/speechbank.htm (accessed July 2005), though this version is not identical to the official text in the Roosevelt Library. It is possible that Roosevelt modified the text as he read it but left the official text as is.

Introduction

1. Freidel, *Franklin D. Roosevelt,* 234.
2. "Letters and cables to Franklin D. Roosevelt." Franklin D. Roosevelt, President's Personal File 200B, Box 11, Franklin D. Roosevelt Library.
3. The term "Fireside Chat" was coined by Harry Butcher of the Columbia Broadcasting System in reference to the second radio address of May 7, 1933. See Lim, "Lion and the Lamb," 438.
4. Moley, *First New Deal,* 22–23.
5. Hamby, *For the Survival of Democracy,* 109.
6. Kennedy, *Freedom from Fear,* 105.
7. Moley, *First New Deal,* 24.
8. Kiewe, "'Whither Bound?'" 56–71.
9. Moley, *First New Deal,* 128.
10. Geret Garrett, "Why Some Banks Fail and Others Don't," reprinted by special permission from the *Saturday Evening Post,* 1933, pp. 3–4, by the Curtis Publishing Co., in Papers of Arthur A. Ballantine, Box 3, Banking Crisis of 1933, Herbert Hoover Presidential Library (hereafter, Hoover Library). Some of the corruption cases involved Samuel Insull's utility holding company in some thirty-two states, which collapsed in 1932, causing major

losses to many investors. Another case was that of Ivar Kreuger, a Swedish financier who cheated bond holders in the United States. See Freidel, *Franklin D. Roosevelt,* 340, 342.

11. Moley, *First New Deal,* 129.
12. In "Constitutionality of Legislation Providing a Unified Commercial Banking System for the United States," Government Printing Office, Washington, 1933, in Arthur A. Ballantine Papers, Box 3, Banking Crisis of 1933, 1933–64, Herbert Hoover Presidential Library.
13. Ballantine, "When All the Banks Closed," 132–33.
14. Rosen, *Hoover, Roosevelt, and the Brains Trust,* 66–67.
15. Cited in ibid., 277.
16. Ibid., 131.
17. Ballantine, "When All the Banks Closed," 133.
18. Ibid., 134.
19. For an excellent discussion of the Hoover's administration view of the gold standard, see Kennedy, *Freedom from Fear,* 75–76.
20. Daigen, "Confidence, Credit, and Cash," 280.
21. Houck, *Rhetoric as Currency,* 1–6. See also McCloskey, *Rhetoric of Economics.*

Chapter 1

1. Brown, *Manipulating the Ether,* 2.
2. Tully, *F. D. R. My Boss,* 88.
3. Sussmann, *Dear FDR,* 74.
4. Ryan, *Franklin D. Roosevelt's Rhetorical Presidency,* 25.
5. Brandenburg and Braden, "Franklin D. Roosevelt's Voice and Pronunciation," 23–24.
6. Hamby, *For the Survival of Democracy,* 79.
7. Oliver, "Speech That Established Roosevelt's Reputation," 274.
8. Crowell, "Franklin D. Roosevelt's Audience Persuasion," 63–64.
9. Brown, *Manipulating the Ether,* 9, 11–14.
10. Sussmann, *Dear FDR,* 112.
11. Ryfe, "Franklin Roosevelt and the Fireside Chats," 82–88, 92–93.
12. Brown, *Manipulating the Ether,* 19.
13. Ryfe, "Franklin Roosevelt and the Fireside Chats," 81–82.
14. "Governor Roosevelt's 'Forgotten Man' Radio Speech, Albany, March 8, 1932," in Rauch, *Roosevelt Reader,* 66.
15. Houck and Kiewe, *FDR's Body Politics.*
16. "Governor Roosevelt's 'Forgotten Man' Radio Speech," 67.
17. Ibid., 67–68.

18. Ibid., 68.
19. Ibid., 68, 69.
20. Ibid., p. 69.

Chapter 2

1. Hamby, *For the Survival of Democracy*, 109–10.
2. Houck, *Rhetoric as Currency*, 168–70.
3. The term "Brain Trust" was coined by reporter James Kiernan of the *New York Times* in reference to Roosevelt's advisers, including Moley, Tugwell, and Adolf A. Berle—all academics who worked together with James Farley, Louis Howe, and Basil O'Connor. See ibid., 117.
4. Rosen, *Hoover, Roosevelt, and the Brains Trust*, 378–79.
5. Houck, *Rhetoric as Currency*, 170.
6. Rosen, *Hoover, Roosevelt, and the Brains Trust*, 378–79.
7. Cited in Houck, *FDR and Fear Itself*, 6.
8. Houck, *Rhetoric as Currency*, 170.
9. Moley, Oral History, entry of January 21, 1933, Hoover Library; and Freidel, *Franklin D. Roosevelt*, 131–32.
10. Moley, Oral History, entry of January 25, 1933.
11. Ibid., entry of January 24, 1933.
12. Moley, the primary speechwriter of Roosevelt's first inaugural address, was quite aware of the various drafts of this address and thus could not see an official from the "money-changers" assuming a prominent position in the Roosevelt administration, and clearly not in the Treasury. See Moley, Oral History, entry of January 25, 1933. In addition, Senator Glass wanted Russell C. Leffingwell, his former assistant and now with Morgan and Company, as his undersecretary. The appointment of the treasury undersecretary would become complicated once Roosevelt decided to keep on Hoover's treasury undersecretary, Arthur A. Ballantine, with whom he also later pleaded to stay longer than he intended. Mr. Ballantine would become the central figure in the banking crisis and primary drafter of the First Fireside Chat.
13. Hamby, *For the Survival of Democracy*, 111.
14. Moley, Oral History, entry of January 28, 1933.
15. Freidel, *Franklin D. Roosevelt*, 36.
16. Ibid., 51.
17. Ibid., 57.
18. Moley, *First New Deal*, 142–43.
19. Freidel, *Franklin D. Roosevelt*, 19.
20. Moley, *First New Deal*, 142–43.
21. Hamby, *For the Survival of Democracy*, 99.

22. Rosen, *Hoover, Roosevelt, and the Brains Trust*, 300.
23. Ibid., 332.
24. Ibid., 301.
25. Ibid., 302.
26. Ibid., 302.
27. Freidel, *Franklin D. Roosevelt*, 18.
28. Moley, *First New Deal*, 144.
29. Freidel, *Franklin D. Roosevelt*, 11.
30. "Hoover to Mills, February 22, 1933," Post Presidential Individual Correspondence, Herbert Hoover Papers. Box 151, Correspondence files of Herbert Hoover with Ogden Mills, Hoover Library.
31. "Hoover to Mills, March 1, 1933," ibid.
32. "Memo, March 2, 1933," Post Presidential Individual Correspondence, Herbert Hoover Papers, Hoover Library.
33. Freidel, *Franklin D. Roosevelt*, 14.
34. Houck, *FDR and Fear Itself*, 80–82, 127.

Chapter 3

1. Freidel, *Franklin D. Roosevelt*, 175.
2. The law required that the Federal Reserve Banks maintain gold reserve in gold or gold certificates of 35 percent against deposit liabilities and 40 percent against liabilities in outstanding Federal Reserve notes. See "The Reminiscences of Walter Wyatt," Oral History Collection, Part IV, 2, Oral History Research Office, Columbia University (hereafter, "Reminiscences of Walter Wyatt").
3. Freidel, *Franklin D. Roosevelt*, 177–79.
4. Houck, *Rhetoric as Currency*, 170.
5. Burns, *Roosevelt*, 146.
6. "Statement of interview with Mr. Henry Ford in Detroit, February 13, 1933, by Secretary Roy D. Chapin and Under Secretary A. A. Ballantine," in Arthur A. Ballantine Papers, Box 3, Banking Crisis of 1933, Hoover Library.
7. Awalt, "Recollection," 357.
8. "Statement of interview with Mr. Henry Ford."
9. Kennedy, *Freedom from Fear*, 132.
10. Quoted in Freidel, *Franklin D. Roosevelt*, 176.
11. Quoted in ibid., 176–77.
12. Herbert Hoover to Senator David A. Reed, February 20, 1933, in Myers and Newton, *Hoover Administration*, 341.
13. Hamby, *For the Survival of Democracy*, 112.
14. "Reminiscences of Walter Wyatt," 3.

15. Freidel, *Franklin D. Roosevelt*, 186.
16. "National Bank Holiday," F. G. Awalt Papers, Box 1, Banking Crisis, Hoover Library.
17. Freidel, *Franklin D. Roosevelt*, 130, 181, 187–88.
18. Ibid., 182–85
19. Ibid., 188, emphasis added.
20. Ibid., 189–90.
21. Ibid., 191.
22. Moley, *First New Deal*, 145–46.
23. "From the diary of Charles S. Hamlin," March 2, 1933, Arthur Ballantine Papers, Box 3, Banking Crisis of 1933, Hoover Library.
24. "Personal Accounts by F. G. Awalt, March 1933, Unpublished," F. G. Awalt Papers, Box 1, Office of the Comptroller, Banking Crisis, Hoover Library.
25. "Outline of Events 3/2/1933–3/4/1933," 1, F. G. Awalt Papers, Box 1, Banking Crisis, Hoover Library.
26. "From the diary of Charles S. Hamlin."
27. "Outline of events 3/2/1933–3/4/1933," 4.
28. "Reminiscences of Walter Wyatt," 4.
29. Since the Federal Reserve in Chicago had "a lot of excess gold," the thought in Washington was to allow Chicago to discount New York's gold reserve. Chicago's Reserve Bank did not wish to discount New York and be told to close its own doors. The compromise was to have the Federal Reserve Banks of New York and Chicago declare bank holidays simultaneously. "Reminiscences of Walter Wyatt," 3–4. The closing of the banks in New York and Chicago made it easier for other state governors, most of them awake around 2 A.M., to close those banks that were still open.
30. Ignoring protocol, Hoover did not invite the president-elect and his wife to dinner but only to tea. See Freidel, *Launching the New Deal*, 192.
31. Moley, Oral History, entry of March 3, 1933.
32. Freidel, *Franklin D. Roosevelt*, 193.
33. Flynn, *Roosevelt Myth*, 26.
34. Moley, *First New Deal*, 151.
35. Moley, Oral History, entry of March 4, 1933.
36. "Outline of events 3/2/1933–3/4/1933," 4–5.
37. Ibid., 6.
38. "Monday night, March 6, 1933," Personal Accounts, F. G. Awalt Papers, Box 1, Hoover Library.

Chapter 4

1. Houck, *FDR and Fear Itself*, 3.
2. For added insight into these divergent rhetorical practices, see Houck, *Rhetoric as Currency*; and McCloskey, *Rhetoric of Economics*.
3. Houck, *FDR and Fear Itself*, 3.
4. Ibid., 4.
5. Ibid., 5.
6. Ibid., 5–7.
7. Moley, *Oral History*, entry of March 5, 1933.
8. Freidel, *Franklin D. Roosevelt*, 217.
9. Ibid., 218–219.
10. "Reminiscences of Walter Wyatt," 15–16.
11. Ibid., 17.
12. Ibid., 15.
13. Historian Lindley traces the use of the Trading with the Enemy Act to a discussion Roosevelt had in January 1933 with Rene Leon, a retired economist who reminded Roosevelt that President Wilson used this act to put an embargo on gold exports during World War I. Roosevelt took this idea to Senator Walsh, his attorney general designate, who was uncertain about it but promised to rule in favor if Roosevelt needed to use it. When Senator Walsh died suddenly on March 2, the new attorney general designate, Homer Cummings, ruled quickly that the 1917 act was valid and could be used to close the banks. Lindley, *Roosevelt Revolution*, 78.
14. "Reminiscences of Walter Wyatt," 27.
15. Cited in Moley, *First New Deal*, 157.
16. Roosevelt, "Proclamation," 1.
17. Roosevelt hoped for only a one-day extension of the bank holiday, but Treasury officials told him that they could not finish assessing all the banks to decide which to open. See Freidel, *Franklin D. Roosevelt*, 229; and Moley, *First New Deal*, 190.
18. Moley, *First New Deal*, 163–64.
19. Freidel, *Franklin D. Roosevelt*, 221.
20. Ibid., 222–223.
21. Roosevelt, "The First Press Conference, March 8, 1933," in Rosenman, *Public Papers and Addresses*, 36.
22. Ibid., 35–36.
23. Ibid., 32.
24. Ibid., 37.
25. Burns, *Roosevelt*, 166.

Chapter 5

1. "Reminiscences of Walter Wyatt," 10.
2. Moley, *First New Deal,* 171.
3. Ibid., 171–73.
4. "Untitled report given to FDR by Ballantine, Woodin and Davidson on March 7, 1933," Arthur Ballantine Papers, Box 3, Banking Crisis of 1933, Hoover Library.
5. Moley, Oral History, entry of March 7, 1933.
6. Ibid.
7. Moley, *First New Deal,* 179.
8. According to Wyatt, Ballantine and Roosevelt knew each other from their Harvard days. See "Reminiscences of Walter Wyatt," 11.
9. Ibid., 21, 23.
10. Ibid., 26.
11. Ibid., 28.
12. Lindley, *Roosevelt Revolution,* 87.
13. Roosevelt's press statement in the *Washington Post,* cited in F. G. Awalt Papers, Awalt's Scrapbook of Bank Crisis, Box 8, Hoover Library.
14. Awalt, "Untitled Memo," Personal Accounts File, part of four items termed confidential and meant for Woodin and dated 3/8, 3/9, 3,16, and 3/24, 1, 5, F. G. Awalt Papers, Box 1, Banking Crisis, Hoover Library.
15. Ibid., 1. Franklin D. Roosevelt, "Message to Congress, March 9, 1933," *Documents and Statements Pertaining to the Banking Emergency,* 2.
16. Awalt, "Untitled Memo," 1. Roosevelt, "Message to Congress, March 9, 1933," 2.
17. Awalt, "Untitled Memo," 3.
18. Ibid., 4. Roosevelt, "Message to Congress, March 9, 1933," 2.
19. Awalt, "Untitled Memo," 5.
20. "Memo, March 6, 1933," Personal Accounts File, F. G. Awalt Papers, Box 1, Banking Crisis, Hoover Library.
21. Ibid.
22. "Reminiscences of Walter Wyatt," 29, 31. Walter Wyatt and his wife witnessed this crucial session.
23. Wyatt claims that the Treasury could not tell the status of state banks and thus could not assess how many of these banks could be opened. See ibid., 32.
24. Lindley, *Roosevelt Revolution,* 87.
25. Moley, *First New Deal,* 183.
26. "Reminiscences of Walter Wyatt," 33.
27. "Telephone conversation—March 10, 1933, 10:30 A.M.," Post Presidential Individual Correspondence, Herbert Hoover Papers, Hoover Library.

28. "Reminiscences of Walter Wyatt," 12.
29. Moley's account of the work of the Hoover Treasury officials in *The First New Deal* was based on Wyatt's input. See "Reminiscences of Walter Wyatt," 18–19.
30. Moley, Oral History, entry of March 12, 1933.
31. Ibid.
32. "Moley to Awalt, February 26, 1964," F. G. Awalt Papers, Box 4, Correspondence, 1933, Hoover Library. Quote from Moley, *First New Deal*, 152.

Chapter 6

1. "Statement by Secretary of the Treasury Woodin, March 9, 1933," F. G. Awalt Papers, Box 1, Banking Crisis, Hoover Library.
2. Ballantine, "When All the Banks Closed," 140.
3. Franklin Roosevelt, "Statement to the Press, March 11, 1933," Washington D.C.: Government Printing Office, 8–9.
4. "Statement by Secretary of the Treasury Woodin, March 13, 1933," F. G. Awalt Papers, Box 1, Banking Crisis, Hoover Library.
5. William Woodin, Secretary of the Treasury, "To the Superintendents of Banks of each State," Government Printing Office, Washington, Part I, February 25–March 31, 1933, *Documents and Statements Pertaining to the Banking Emergency*, 18 [17–18].
6. Freidel, *Franklin D. Roosevelt*, 230.
7. Brown, *Manipulating the Ether*, 17.
8. Brandenburg, "Franklin D. Roosevelt's International Speeches," 26.
9. Moley, *First New Deal*, 194. Burns, *Fox and the Lion*, 140.
10. Michelson, *Ghost Talks*, 56–57.
11. The drafting of the First Fireside Chat was attributed to Moley so many times that he paid special attention to this issue, clarifying Michelson's initial work on the speech and Ballantine's rewriting of the speech. See Moley, *After Seven Years*, 155.
12. Ballantine had dabbled in speechwriting earlier, drafting speeches for Hoover. See note of appreciation Ballantine sent Hoover after the latter thanked him for his work, including the drafting of speeches; "Ballantine to Hoover, February 28, 1933," Arthur Ballantine Papers, Box 3, Banking Crisis of 1933, Hoover Library. Also see Moley, *First New Deal*, 194.
13. Michelson, *Ghost Talks*, 56–57.
14. "Wyatt to Ballantine, August 1, 1944," Arthur Ballantine Papers, Box 3, Banking Crisis, Hoover Library.
15. Ibid.
16. Ballantine, "Ghost and the Banks," 18.

17. "Notes on conversation with Goldenweiser, re: Bank Holiday, August 1, 1944," Arthur Ballantine Papers, Box 3, Banking Crisis 1933, Hoover Library.
18. Flynn, *Roosevelt Myth*, 31.
19. Freidel, *Franklin D. Roosevelt*, 230.
20. Awalt, "Recollections," 371.
21. Ibid.
22. "Letters and cables to Franklin D. Roosevelt." President's Personal File 200B, Box 8A–B; Box 9B–J; Box 10K–S; Box 11S–Z, Franklin D. Roosevelt Library.
23. This account was given to me by Roosevelt Library archivist Alycia J. Vivona, via e-mail, August 11, 2004.
24. The printed copy of the First Fireside Chat that exists in the Master Speech File in the Franklin D. Roosevelt Library contains only two minor modifications by Roosevelt. One has to assume that Roosevelt made these modifications shortly before or shortly after he read the speech. The file also contains handwritten notes explaining why the original reading copy is missing. The first note cites Ray Moley's *After Seven Years*, 155, "for comments on drafting of this speech (March 12, 1933)," and the second note cites Grace Tully's *FDR, My Boss*, 92, "about disappearance of reading copy." The notes were added in 1956 and 1958, respectively, probably by a library archivist.
25. Hurd, *When the New Deal*, 248.
26. Burns, *Roosevelt*, 167–68.
27. Franklin D. Roosevelt, Fireside Chat, Number One, The Banking Crisis, March 12, 1933, Master Speech File, No. 616a, Franklin D. Roosevelt Library. Page numbers cited in the remainder of this chapter refer to this file.
28. Brown, *Manipulating the Ether*, 18.
29. Brandenburg, "Franklin D. Roosevelt's International Speeches," 36–37.
30. The word "temporarily" was added to the text, but it does not appear to be in Roosevelt's handwriting.
31. Roosevelt had a penchant for using war or military metaphors in his speeches, thus projecting the need for cooperation and action from the American people in times of urgency and consequently "garnering unified support." The use of the war metaphor also alluded to the promise of victory, by asking people to "fight back." See Daughton, "Metaphorical Transcendence," 430–32.
32. Houck and Kiewe, *FDR's Body Politics*.
33. Campbell, *Rhetorical Act*, 33.
34. Ryfe, "Franklin Roosevelt and the Fireside Chats," 93.
35. Ryan, *Franklin D. Roosevelt's Rhetorical Presidency*, 19–21.

Chapter 7

1. Burns, *Roosevelt*, 181.
2. Flynn, *Roosevelt Myth*, 31.
3. Freidel, *Franklin D. Roosevelt*, 230.
4. Burns, *Roosevelt*, 205.
5. Kennedy, *Freedom from Fear*, 137.
6. Moley, *After Seven Years*, 155.
7. "Reminiscences of Walter Wyatt," 18–19.
8. Ibid., 34.
9. Ibid., 63.
10. Ballantine, "When All the Banks Closed," 140.
11. In 1947, congressional testimony of RFC operation indicated that, of the total $3.3 billion put out by the RFC, $3 billion had been repaid and that the net loss to the government was around $125 million. See ibid., 140–41.
12. Kennedy, *Freedom from* Fear, 137.
13. Unless otherwise cited, all letters are from Franklin D. Roosevelt, President's Personal File 200B, Boxes 8, 9, 10, 11, Franklin D. Roosevelt Library.
14. Levine and Levine, *People and the President*, 2–3.
15. Ibid., 3.
16. Quoted in Ryan, *Franklin D. Roosevelt's Rhetorical Presidency*, 32.
17. Levine and Levine, *People and the President*, 38–39.
18. Ibid., 39.
19. Ibid., 41–42.
20. Ibid., 41.
21. Ibid., 42.
22. F. G. Awalt Papers, Clippings from Newspapers, Scrapbook of Banking Crisis, Box 8, Hoover Library. The newspapers in this file are not always identified.
23. Cited in Freidel, *Franklin D. Roosevelt*, 236.
24. Follet, "Remembered Man," 129, 137.
25. Hauser, *Vernacular Voices*, 238–39.

Chapter 8

1. Alter, "What FDR Teaches Us," 29.
2. "Roosevelt to Ballantine, March 28, 1933," Arthur Ballantine Papers, Banking Crisis of 1933, Box 3, Hoover Library.
3. "Memorandum of April 14, 1933," Arthur Ballantine Papers, Banking Crisis of 1933, Box 3, Hoover Library.

4. "Roosevelt to Ballantine, May 15, 1933," Arthur Ballantine Papers, Banking Crisis of 1933, Box 3, Hoover Library.

5. Ballantine, "Ghost and the Banks," 18.

6. "Woodin to Ballantine, June 14, 1933," Arthur Ballantine Papers, Box 3, Banking Crisis of 1933, Hoover Library.

7. Unidentified newspaper clipping, with no date given, Arthur Ballantine Papers, Banking Crisis of 1933, Hoover Library.

8. Ballantine, "Ghost and the Banks," 18.

9. *New York Times,* June 28, 1933, Arthur Ballantine Papers, clipping in Box 3, Banking Crisis of 1933, Hoover Library.

10. "Treasury Refuses Detroit Bank Data," *New York Times,* July 9, 1933, no page cited, Arthur Ballantine Papers, newspaper clippings in Box 3, Banking Crisis of 1933, Hoover Library.

11. "Ballantine to Chapin, August 16, 1934," Arthur Ballantine Papers, Box 3, Banking Crisis of 1933, Hoover Library.

12. Ballantine, "When All the Banks Closed," 144.

13. Historian Alonzo Hamby makes this claim. See *For the Survival of Democracy,* 112.

14. Freidel, *Franklin D. Roosevelt,* 334.

15. Ibid., 195.

16. Burns, *Roosevelt,* 168.

Bibliography

Manuscript Sources

Arthur A. Ballantine Papers, Herbert Hoover Presidential Library, West Branch, Iowa.

F. G. Awalt Papers, Herbert Hoover Presidential Library, West Branch, Iowa.

Herbert Hoover Papers, Herbert Hoover Presidential Library, West Branch, Iowa.

Letters and cables to Franklin D. Roosevelt, President's Personal File, Franklin D. Roosevelt Library, Hyde Park, N.Y.

Moley, Raymond, Oral History, Herbert Hoover Presidential Library, West Branch, Iowa.

"The Reminiscences of Walter Wyatt," Oral History Collection, Oral History Research Office, Columbia University. Based on an oral interview conducted by James E. Sargent in Washington D.C., May 18, 1970. Microfilm.

Roosevelt, Franklin D., Master Speech File, Franklin D. Roosevelt Library, Hyde Park, N.Y.

Published Sources

Alter, Jonathan. "What FDR Teaches Us," *Newsweek,* May 1, 2006, 29.

Awalt, F. Gloyd. "Recollection of the Banking Crisis in 1933." *Business History Review* 43 (Autumn 1969): 347–71.

Ballantine, Arthur A. "When All the Banks Closed." *Harvard Business Review* 26 (March 1948): 129–43.

———. "The Ghost and the Banks." *Herald Tribune,* August 23, 1944, 18.

Brandenburg, Earnest. "Franklin D. Roosevelt's International Speeches, 1939–1941." *Speech Monograph* 16 (1949): 21–40.

———, and Waldo W. Braden. "Franklin D. Roosevelt's Voice and Pronunciation." *Quarterly Journal of Speech* 38 (1952): 23–30.

Brown, Robert J. *Manipulating the Ether: The Power of Broadcast Radio in Thirties America.* Jefferson, N.C.: McFarland, 1998.

Buhite, Russel D., and David W. Levy, eds. *FDR's Fireside Chats*. Norman: University of Oklahoma Press, 1992.

Burns, James MacGregor. *Roosevelt: The Lion and the Fox*. New York: Harcourt, Brace, 1956.

Campbell, Karlyn Kohrs. *The Rhetorical Act*. Belmont, Calif.: Wadsworth, 1982

Crowell, Laura. "Franklin D. Roosevelt's Audience Persuasion in the 1936 Campaign." *Speech Monograph* 17 (1950): 48–64.

Daigen, J. M. "Confidence, Credit, and Cash: Shall We Guarantee Them in Our Banks?" *Harper Magazine* 166 (March 1933): 278–92.

Daughton, Suzanne M. "Metaphorical Transcendence Images of the Holy War in Franklin Roosevelt's First Inaugural." *Quarterly Journal of Speech* 79 (1993): 427–46.

Documents and Statements Pertaining to the Banking Emergency. Presidential Proclamations, Federal Legislation, Executive Orders, Regulations, and other Documents, Part I, February 25–March 31, 1933. Washington D.C.: Government Printing Office.

Flynn, John T. *The Roosevelt Myth*. New York: Devin-Adair, 1956.

Follet, Wilson, "The Remembered Man to His President." *Atlantic Monthly* 152 (August 1933): 129–37.

Freidel, Frank. *Franklin D. Roosevelt: Launching the New Deal*. Boston Little, Brown, 1973.

Gordon, George N., and Irving A. Falk. *On-the-Spot Reporting: Radio Records History*. New York: Julian Messner, 1967.

Hamby, Alonzo L. *For the Survival of Democracy: Franklin Roosevelt and the World Crisis of the 1930s*. New York: Free Press, 2004.

Hauser, Gerard A. *Vernacular Voices: The Rhetoric of Publics and Public Spheres*. Columbia: University of South Carolina Press, 1999.

Houck, Davis W. *Rhetoric as Currency: Hoover, Roosevelt and the Great Depression*. College Station: Texas A&M University Press, 2001.

———. *FDR and Fear Itself: The First Inaugural Address*. College Station: Texas A&M University Press, 2002.

———, and Amos Kiewe. *FDR's Body Politics: The Rhetoric of Disability*. College Station: Texas A&M Press, 2003.

Hurd, Charles. *When the New Deal Was Young and Gay*. New York: Hawthorn Books, 1965.

Kennedy, David M. *Freedom from Fear: The American People in Depression and War, 1929–1945*. New York: Oxford University Press, 1999.

Kiewe, Amos. "'Whither Bound?' Franklin D. Roosevelt's 'Quo Vadis,'" *Southern Communication Journal* 70 (2004): 56–71.

Levine, Lawrence W., and Cornelia R. Levine. *The People and the President: America's Conversation with FDR*. Boston: Beacon Press, 2002.

Lim, Elvin T. "The Lion and the Lamb: De-mythologizing Franklin Roosevelt's Fireside Chats." *Rhetoric and Public Affairs* 6 (2003): 437–64.

Lindley, Ernest K. *The Roosevelt Revolution: First Phase.* New York: Viking Press, 1933.

McCloskey, Donald N. *The Rhetoric of Economics.* Madison: University of Wisconsin Press, 1985.

Michelson, Charles. *The Ghost Talks.* New York: G. P. Putnam's Sons, 1944.

Moley, Raymond. *After Seven Years.* New York: Harper & Brothers, 1939.

———. *The First New Deal.* New York: Harcourt, Brace & World, 1966.

Myers, William Starr, and Walter H. Newton. *The Hoover Administration: A Documented Narrative.* New York: Scribners, 1936.

Oliver, Robert T. "The Speech That Established Roosevelt's Reputation." *Quarterly Journal of Speech* 31 (1945): 274–82.

Rauch, Basil, ed. *The Roosevelt Reader: Selected Speeches, Messages, Press Conferences, and Letters of Franklin D. Roosevelt.* New York: Holt, Reinhart and Winston, 1964.

Rosen, Eliot A. *Hoover, Roosevelt, and the Brains Trust: From Depression to New Deal.* New York: Columbia University Press, 1977.

Rosenman, Samuel I., ed. *The Public Papers and Addresses of Franklin D. Roosevelt,* Vol. 2. New York: Random House, 1938.

Ryan, Halford R. *Franklin D. Roosevelt's Rhetorical Presidency.* Westport, Conn.: Greenwood Press, 1988.

Ryfe, David M. "Franklin Roosevelt and the Fireside Chats." *Journal of Communication* 49 (1999): 80–103.

Sussmann, Leila A. *Dear FDR: A Study of Political Letter-Writing.* Totowa, N.J.: Bedminster Press, 1963.

Tully, Grace. *F. D. R. My Boss.* New York: Charles Scribner's Sons, 1949.

Index